The Girl Refused

C000121603

by
Cassie Farren

Welford Publishing

Published in 2016 by Welford Publishing

Copyright © Cassie Farren 2016

2nd Edition
First published by Welford Publishing in 2014

ISBN: Paperback 978-0-9931296-2-9
ISBN: ebook 978-0-9931296-3-6

Front cover photograph © Donna Eade 2014
Author photograph © Kate Sharp Photography 2016

A catalogue record for this book is available
from the British Library

Published with the help of Indie Authors World

IndieAuthors
World

For Kieron & Lennie

You always have been, and always will be,
my inspiration never to give up. xx

The Girl Who Refused To Quit

If your life has taken an unexpected downturn; if you feel that life isn't fair; if you have lost your way, or lost hope it will get better – then **read this book**. Cassie writes with honesty as she shares her inspiring journey through the ups and downs of her life. Her story of facing, accepting, and finding ways to overcome real life difficulties, disappointment, self-doubt and worry, will give you a new perspective and insight into how you, too, can refuse to quit.

Kim Macleod, Author of *From Heartbreak to Happiness.*

As I turned the pages, Cassie's story began to run through my veins as if it were my own. As the chapters progressed, I felt myself holding back the tears with a lump in my throat. It all felt very personal somehow, like it was my own story.
Cassie uses her own pain and struggles to help others; she touches home so closely that you feel moved beyond words. Cassie has a magic that transpires the page and I believe that anyone who reads this book will feel it.
The Girl Who Refused To Quit has left me with lessons for life I will never forget.

Katy Summers

Cassie has written a heart-warming book with honesty and a bundle of true inspiration. It reminds you to trust your inner voice and that as one door shuts another opens. Wherever you are in your life currently, all readers will be able to take some great nuggets of inspiration from this book.

Marie Clarke

The Girl Who Refused To Quit is an absorbing read right from the start. Cassie's story hooks you in straight away.

If you're feeling directionless, isolated, and trying to figure out who you are, you are not alone!

It's in times of trouble it helps to look inside of yourself, but sometimes it pays to look outside of your own life and see how others have coped. Where to turn to? Reading Cassie Farren's journey against the odds to build a successful business and career is one of the wiser places to start. An inspiring read.

Steph Robson, The Business Groove

One word… WOW! This book tells a story of all the experiences, realities and obstacles many women face in adult life. It's powerful, moving and, most importantly, has given me a massive kick in the backside to just deal with the stuff I have had to deal with and move on. If any ladies out there are stuck, be it in a negative relationship or career or feel their passion, drive, determination and will has got up and walked out, then this is the book for you.

A true from-the-heart read, and I recommend it to all ladies who are mums, trying to do their best and searching for that 'there's more to life than this'!

Anita McAloren

About the Author

Cassie, who lives in Northamptonshire, England, has been described as "the girl next door who wants the best of both worlds". Her priority has always been the happiness and security of her family, and she cherishes the moments and the memories they make in the quality time they spend together. Cassie loves being around the special people in her life, relaxing in the countryside, and exploring new places.

Cassie wants to inspire other women to live their life fearlessly, and to never give up. She is not your typical businesswoman with years of experience and numerous degrees under her belt, but believes what she has gained through real life experience is invaluable and can benefit others. Having turned her own life around, Cassie now takes great pride in helping other women to live the life they know they deserve.

Acknowledgements

I would like to thank my parents and my sister for their unconditional love and support.

Thank you to my true friends. Through the laughter and the tears on this crazy journey, your friendship has been invaluable.

Thank you to Kim and Sinclair Macleod from Indie Authors World for making the production of my book an enjoyable and stress-free process.

Thank you to Christine McPherson for your help, knowledge, and support in editing my book.

Thank you to the Northamptonshire Enterprise Partnership for having confidence in me and seeing the vision for my business.

Thank you to Dave O'Connor for the important part you have played in my journey, and which led me to find my true path.

Thank you to Sandie. I apologise for laughing when you first told me I should set up my own business, you were right!

Poem by Cassie

Your questions have no answers,
You feel lost, alone, and afraid.
Your head is spinning endlessly
As life passes in a daze.

It's time to trust your instincts,
Allow your pain and the darkness to fade.
Your lessons are ready to unfold now,
They will guide you day by day.

No anger or regrets will consume you
As you find the strength to move on.
Your voice and the strength within you
Were with you all along.

Hold your head high, live life on your terms.
You can do this, it's time to commit.
Know you're worthy, take one step at a time.

From

The Girl Who Refused To Quit.

Introduction

I was never one of those girls who had her life planned out years in advance, knowing exactly what job she was going to have, what house she was going to live in, or her colour-co-ordinated wedding scrapbook in hand before she'd met the man of her dreams! And I'm glad that I didn't. If I had set such high expectations, I know I would have felt like even more of a failure.

I can now look back over the years and piece together the events that have led me to be where I am today. Was it fate? Was it all meant to be? One thing I know for sure is that I had some serious lessons to learn. You may be wondering why I am letting you into my world. As I type this now, knowing that the words on my computer screen will be made into a book, I feel scared. I know it would be easier to keep quiet, smile sweetly, and pretend it never happened. But I can't do that; my instincts are too strong to fight.

If sharing my journey can help just one other person to realise that no matter what happens in their life they do not have to be defined by their circumstances, they can hold their head high, and they too can make that decision to refuse to quit, then I know it will be worth it.

Cassie

> *"And the day came when the risk it took to remain tightly closed in a bud was more painful that the risk it took to blossom." Anais Nin*

Chapter 1

I couldn't breathe. My legs felt like lead as I tried to climb the stairs. I couldn't fight it, the grief took over and my legs collapsed beneath me. I couldn't see for the tears that were streaming down my face as I sat sobbing halfway up the stairs. I knew from the physical pain I could feel in my heart that the last hour of my life had not been a dream, but a living nightmare that was about to change my life as I knew it. Part of me wanted to scream and shout, the other part wanted to go to sleep and wake up when all the pain had gone. Would it ever go?

The phone call I'd made to my parents ten minutes before was the hardest I have ever had to make. I can recall my mum answering in her positive and cheery voice, asking if I was okay, but I can't remember the words that came out of my mouth. I vividly remember the most awful gut-wrenching feeling that I had let my parents down. They had done a fantastic job bringing up me and my sister; there had never been any pressure to bring home endless degrees or pursue a certain career, all they ever wanted was for us to be happy. This conversation was about to change that.

My voice quivered as I told my mum that something had happened which I couldn't accept. I had ended my relationship and was going to be living on my own with my six-month-old son, Kieron. My head was spinning and my heart was pounding, but I didn't have time to wallow in self-pity. My life was slowly collapsing around me and I needed to make some quick decisions.

I knew I was going to lose a lot, and the future wasn't going to be easy bringing up Kieron on my own. But in the chaos of my mind there was something that was crystal clear – I was determined not to lose my house. I would never have chosen to live on my own, but I couldn't face the added stress and worry of moving to a different area, not knowing if it was safe. Protective of Kieron, I was scared of being rehoused in an area that I wasn't familiar with. My family didn't live in the same town and couldn't just pop round if I was worried or if I heard strange noises in the night. I also knew I was going to be spending a lot of time in the house and, when Kieron spent time with his dad, I would be there alone. I decided then and there that I would do whatever it took to keep that roof over both of our heads.

My parents were as devastated as me; they were shocked and upset, no-one had expected this. The next decision I had to make was one that some mothers agonise over for months, but I had to make mine in a matter of minutes. I asked my mum if she could look after Kieron for two days in the week. I had recently returned to work part-time but now I would need to return to work full time as soon as possible. I knew the nursery he attended wouldn't be able to accommodate the two extra days for at least another six months, but I would need a full time salary to enable me to buy Kieron's dad out of our house.

My mum agreed without hesitation, and said that both her and my dad would do whatever they could to support me. I felt bad that they were so upset, but I knew I had to try and hold things together. I was really grateful for their help but knew it wasn't going to be easy. It was going to mean driving a sixty mile round trip to take and collect Kieron each time, in between working full time. I reminded myself to look at the bigger picture, and made the next phone call to my boss to ask if I could return to work full time immediately. I couldn't get through, so knew I'd need to speak her face-to-face at work in the morning.

I don't know how long it took me to walk up the stairs that night, but as I reached the top I found myself gazing into Kieron's bedroom looking at his tiny face – so peaceful and innocent – as he slept. Through my tears, I whispered to him over and over, "I'm so sorry, I'm so sorry."

Would he ever forgive me for making this decision? Would he hate me? Had I done the right thing? Those were the thoughts that ran through my head as I finally fell asleep on my tear-stained pillow.

***

I drove into work in a daze the next morning. I arrived in body, but I'm not sure where my head was, and went to get a cup of tea. My boss saw me and apologised for missing my call, then took one look at my face and asked if everything was alright. My bottom lip trembled as I mumbled that I wasn't alright, and the tears returned again. Thankfully, she agreed that I could return to work full time. I was so relieved, though still worried and scared about how I would cope with everything. I was sent home that day, as I wasn't in a fit state to work.

Chapter 2

I don't know if it was a good idea to be left alone with my own thoughts. I reflected back on when I had first moved out of my parents' house, to begin a new life with Kieron's dad. Everything had been going so well. I'd found a new job, had two promotions, and we'd bought our new house .We both wanted children, and decided the time was right to start a family.

Finding out you are pregnant is a really surreal time. I was so happy, at the same time I was absolutely petrified! There was a baby alive inside me; I felt so protective already. I was responsible for this little life until he was born, and then for all of his life. I hardly knew anyone that had a baby at my age.

I was only 22, and even though we had been together for a while, many people took great pleasure in telling me I was far too young to be a mum. They kept asking if it was what I wanted, shouldn't I be travelling or at university and enjoying myself? I really wanted to tell them to mind their own business, but I remained polite and replied that it was what we both wanted and that we were looking forward to becoming parents.

Of course, this was only the beginning of other people letting me know their opinion – my pregnant body appeared to become public property! Over the next few months I seemed to attract almost daily comments from people, asking how much weight had I put on, what size was I, was I going to have a natural birth? Would I breastfeed? Was my baby planned? Did I have any stretch marks!? The pregnancy magazines certainly don't warn you about the constant intrusion of your privacy! One woman asked me if I knew whether I was having a boy or a girl. When I replied happily that I was having a boy, she got in a mood and said she didn't want to know and that I had spoiled her surprise! What on earth was that about?

Everyone seemed to have some comment about my grow-ing body. I had always been fairly slim so it was almost like people were happy I was getting bigger. I would be told, "Wow, you're massive!" or "Have you got two in there?" A lot of the time these comments were from people I barely knew. I know that most of them didn't mean to offend me, but any woman who has been pregnant will understand that it can be a very sensitive time.

As I grew bigger I started to lose confidence, and the running body commentary really didn't help. I was fully aware that I was growing a baby and how important it was to reach full term, but it didn't stop me questioning why some people were so insensitive.

Another topic they don't cover in the pregnancy magazines is how you will cope with being in labour. I had numerous women desperate to share their horror stories with a first-time mum with no idea what to expect. I kept telling them (and myself) that there was no-one that could tell me how I would cope, so it was almost irrelevant worrying about how traumatic it could be.

When my contractions started at about 2pm, I remained calm, kept an open mind about pain relief, and reminded myself that this pain was self-inflicted! I was going to be in a hospital with pain relief available to me and I knew that as soon as my son arrived, the pain was going to stop. As my contractions progressed, I paced the house so much it's a wonder I didn't wear the carpets out. I had so many baths I'm surprised I didn't look like a shrivelled-up apricot, but my appearance was the last thing on my mind!

I stayed at home as long as I could, until at 3am we went to the hospital. I had heard of so many people having false alarms and being sent home, and was silently praying this wasn't the case. The pain was so bad that I couldn't speak when I had a contraction – surely this must be the real thing! I left my bags in the car just in case I was still in the early stages, and made my way to labour ward.

The midwife came to see me, confirmed I definitely was in labour, and informed me that I only had a few hours left before I would having my baby! A very surprised voice came out of my mouth: "Shall I bring my bags in from the car now?" The midwife was laughing as she asked me about my labour plan. Labour plan? I was still getting over the shock that I was in labour and would be going home with a baby! I told her about my numerous baths and asked if I could I try their birthing pool. I would get out at any time if I wanted any pain relief.

I remember walking up what seemed like a never-ending corridor, bent over double with each contraction, and thinking, "So this is why they call it labour!" I had no idea how I was going to cope over the next few hours if the pain became more intense, but I was amazed when I got into the water birth pool and felt the amazing pain relief. I felt like I had rewound in time with the level of pain; my contractions still hurt, but I felt calm and in control as I bobbed around in the pool with a swimming pool woggle and a cup of water!

Kieron was born two hours later in the birthing pool. There was no way I was getting out of that pool for neither love nor money! If it was possible to bottle the feeling of that last contraction leaving your body as you meet your baby for the first time, you could sell it for a million pounds or more! Nothing could have prepared me for the overwhelming love that I felt in that moment, combined with the relief that the pain had ended.

Everything I had planned for the last nine months suddenly became an overwhelming reality, the emotional journey of becoming a parent had begun.

Chapter 3

The weeks and months after Kieron was born, were a blur of sheer exhaustion. A good night consisted of three hours' broken sleep, and a bad night meant none. I resorted to sleeping on the sofa through the night and walking around like a zombie through the day. I loved being a mum – it was so rewarding, but the exhaustion was like nothing I had ever known.

Women are encouraged to adopt healthy eating habits once their baby is born, but there were some days I would forget to eat at all. A hot cup of tea became a distant memory, and I would eat the quickest food available, regardless of the vitamin content. I was planning to return to work when Kieron was six months old and, despite how shattered I was, I wanted to get back to feeling like the old me. It had been far too long since I'd felt good about myself. For months I had been wearing oversized clothes and baggy jumpers and this wasn't helping my already lowered self-esteem.

Once I joined a gym and started making healthier choices, I did see a difference. Five months passed and I was still struggling to shift my last stone of extra baby weight. I would see all these 'yummy mummies' in magazines and on the television, looking gorgeous and slim in what seemed like days after having their children. I felt uncomfortable being bigger and just wanted my old body back. My confidence had already decreased as a result of not working for the first time in my life. But I was doing the hardest and most important job I had ever done – I was on call 24 hours a day; I was constantly sleep deprived; and I felt like I had no value.

I only had one month left on maternity leave before I was due to go back to work part time, and I wanted to fit into my work clothes again. Common sense went out of the window and some days I would live on cups of instant soup, or I would skip meals completely in a bid to lose that final baby weight. It didn't work, and in fact I would get so hungry that I would binge on junk food and then feel really crap for letting myself down again.

I remember one day walking into town and being so hungry that I bought three chocolate bars and they were all eaten before I got back home! It was a relentless and exhausting cycle, and I had forgotten what it felt like to feel normal. Friends would visit and tell me I looked great but somehow it just didn't register. I wasn't happy with my weight or how I looked, and unfortunately no amount of "You're looking well" compliments were going to change that.

The day came when I was going to be returning to work for three days a week. I had been off for over six months and had already lost a sense of purpose, so I went back to work feeling like I didn't know who I was. I felt so stupid. How on earth could I lose myself on maternity leave? Having a baby was meant to be one of the happiest times in my life.

Any mum who has returned to work after having a baby can relate to the uncertainty and mixed emotions that come with it. I had become an expert in quick nappy changes, preparing milk feeds, and running round like a crazy lady doing housework in the short time whilst Kieron slept. But the girl who was the expert in spreadsheets and negotiating prices eight months ago was nowhere to be seen. Would I even remember my job role? Would Kieron get on okay being left at a nursery for three days a week? Was it possible to arrive at work on time without milk stains down my suit?

Unbeknown to me, these would prove to be the least of my worries.

Just four weeks after I returned to work, my world crumbled, and I found myself facing that struggle to walk up the stairs, blinded by my tears. None of us knows exactly what will happen in our lives, but being a single mum aged 23 was certainly never in my plans. I was devastated, humiliated, and had no idea how I was going to cope.

I'd been brought up in a very loving and secure family. My parents both had good jobs, my sister had graduated from university and started her career, I'd worked hard at school and college and left with a good level of education. I had a happy childhood and still look back at fond memories of our holidays and days out, and enjoyed being part of a secure family unit. There was never any doubt in my mind that I wanted to bring Kieron up in the same way. I just hadn't thought about doing it as a single mum.

Although I had a good circle of friends, I had never felt so lonely. The majority of my friends had gone to university and were doing well in their careers. I didn't know many people my age that were mums, let alone single mums.

My head would go into overdrive. Were people laughing at me behind my back? Were they thinking, "We told you so, you were too young to have a baby and now look what's happened!" Were people watching me, waiting for me to crumble? They were irrational thoughts, but the shock and despair of the reality I faced would often feed the negative committee that gathered in my head. If I had opened up and spoken to people about my worries maybe I could have put things into perspective, but I felt like I just had to keep going and try and keep my head in the right place. I rarely spoke about how I felt to anyone. I wanted to do the best that I could for Kieron and avoid any unnecessary stress, which meant keeping our house.

Once I returned to work full time, I made an appointment with a mortgage advisor. On the outside I was calmly answering his questions and making polite chit-chat. On the inside my heart was pounding and the voice in my head was stuck on repeat, praying, "Please let this go through. Please let this go through!" If I could borrow enough money to buy Kieron's dad out of the house, it would mean I could keep our home, which would be a huge weight off my mind.

As we reached the end of the mortgage interview, I heard the advisor say, "I have got one more question for you." I was panicking and trying not to scream out loud, "Please just agree my mortgage!" So I was shocked to hear the words, "I know you have a lot going on at the moment, Cassie, but I'd like to offer you a job." I was stunned; I had only gone in for a mortgage!

The company offered to pay for me to study for my CeMAP (Certificate in Mortgage Advice and Practice) qualifications and, once I had qualified, I would have my own branch. The advisor suggested I go away and think about it and let him know my decision. But I decided then and there that I wanted to accept. Yes, I did have a lot going on; yes, I may have been slightly mad, but in that moment I felt a very small flicker of ambition reignite inside me.

My first ever job – before I relocated – had been in a building society, and I had really enjoyed it. Taking my official mortgage qualifications would mean I could work towards something that could make a positive impact on our future. Maybe this was the chance I needed. I reminded myself it wasn't going to easy, but I knew it would be worth it. I would be at home most evenings, so I could study for my qualifications once Kieron was in bed.

I knew this would give me a sense of purpose, something to aim towards. So I handed in my notice at my old job and dug deep for some fresh brain cells that were going to take a huge pounding over the next few months!

When my personal mortgage was agreed, I was elated – and so relieved we could begin our new life.

Chapter 4

From the outside looking in, most people would have said that I was coping quite well considering the huge life changes I had undergone. Having a baby was stressful; becoming a first time mum was stressful; going back to work was stressful. Added to that, becoming a single mum was stressful, going to back to work full time was stressful, and hardly seeing my son was stressful. Starting a new career was stressful; studying for new qualifications was stressful. I had endured all of these in a very short space of time – and the cracks were beginning to show.

I was mentally and physically exhausted, and on the slippery slope to a bad place. The pressure took its toll as I began to hate myself and my body. My tired mind, which had once been calm and serene, now felt tangled and confused as it searched for the answers I couldn't find. How had my life ended up like this? What was wrong with me? When would it get easier?

I felt like I wasn't good enough and that I had failed Kieron. Having gone from struggling to lose weight a few months earlier, I now found that the weight had started to fall off me. I was hungry but I could barely eat. Kieron would have all his meals at nursery so he was fine, but I found it depressing working all day to then come home and cook a meal for one.

One Sunday I felt really positive and decided to cook myself a roast dinner. I went to the supermarket and bought the ingredients, then spent all afternoon in the kitchen preparing and cooking my roast chicken dinner for one. When I finally sat down to eat it, I just burst out crying. This wasn't how it was meant to be. I felt sad and alone, envious of all the families that would be sitting down together, surrounded by loved ones, enjoying their family meal. No doubt someone would be pointlessly moaning that they wanted crispier roast potatoes or bickering over who was having the chicken legs, but they had no idea how lucky they were.

My life consisted of looking after Kieron, working full time, and studying in the evenings for my exams. I was beyond exhausted. I went into work a few times having had about two hours sleep when Kieron was suffering dreaded teething pain. I longed for a break. Yet when I was on my own I missed my little boy so much, the house felt too quiet, and I wanted him to be with me again.

My weight fell drastically to less than 8 stones over the next few months. I looked gaunt and withdrawn, and I had zero confidence. But the crazy voice inside my head was telling me I was fat and ugly. I couldn't see the reality of the situation, my head was in such a mess, and I hated the reflection staring back at me in the mirror. I didn't know whether to laugh or cry when my mum bought me a new T-shirt. It was bright pink with "I'm gorgeous" written in sparkly silver diamantes! There was no way I was going to be wearing that! I could see my mum was a bit upset. She told me that I was gorgeous but my mind was telling me, "Well, you're my mum, so you would say that."

**

The day I knew something had to change was when I went into a shop to try on some new jeans. I stared at my reflection in disbelief as the pair that fitted me perfectly were a size 8. I had walked into that changing room convinced that I was fat, ugly, and worthless. I realised then that there was nothing wrong with my body, but there was something wrong with my mind.

I looked at myself in the mirror and silently told myself I needed to sort it out. It was time to stop punishing myself. If I believed that I wasn't good enough, I was never going to move on with my life.

I was determined not to let the ghosts of my past deny the happiness of my future. I threw away my bathroom scales (sometimes I had checked my weight three times a day!) and, over 10 years later, I haven't owned another set.

Slowly I started to pick up the pieces of my life. I threw myself into my career by studying for my exams, and I was so proud when my hard work paid off. I passed every exam first time and six months later was a very proud, fully qualified mortgage advisor.

I appreciate that mortgages aren't everyone's cup of tea but I loved playing a part in what can be a very daunting and stressful time in someone's life. I enjoyed explaining everything to them in a way they could understand, and was pleased when my work could help enable them to move into their dream house. I found it very rewarding and enjoyed the rapport and professional relationship that I built with the clients. I was feeling positive about the future –things were looking up.

Unfortunately, this positivity was short-lived. I discovered that my employers were experiencing financial difficulty, and I became worried when I began to receive my wages late. Living alone, with an increased mortgage and high nursery fees to pay, was hard to manage. I knew that if I ever defaulted on my own mortgage payment, there would be little point in applying for a job anywhere else as a mortgage advisor due to the very strict credit checks.

When my pay cheque was late for the third consecutive month, the stress got too much and I reluctantly handed in my notice. My boss called the owner of the company, and relayed the message back to me that I was to collect my mortgage certificates and leave the branch immediately. I was in shock. I'd expected to have a month to look for another job and to make a plan.

I said goodbye to everyone, collected my certificates, and walked out of the branch in floods of tears. What had I done? I felt like I'd been forced into this situation. I couldn't risk not getting paid on time, with the ongoing stress of potentially defaulting on my bills. I felt scared and angry as I sent my CV to every bank that had a vacancy and hoped I would find another job as soon as possible.

It wasn't long before I had some interviews, and I was so happy and relieved to be offered a job at a high street bank. I felt really positive about working for a large company. At least I knew they were definitely going to pay me on time, and I was looking forward to having the chance to apply for promotions and progress within the company in the future.

Frustratingly, it took six months from my initial interview until I walked into the bank on my first day! There was endless paperwork, references, and checks to do before I could begin, so I was forced to endure a challenging six months of temporary work. It meant taking a pay cut, the work wasn't guaranteed, and even though I was grateful to be employed the jobs were mind-numbing and tedious.

During that time, I spent a few months at a call centre making cold calls all day every day. It was so degrading having employers look down their nose at you, fellow colleagues would judge you, and customers would be rude and obnoxious. But it wasn't a time to be fussy. My bills needed to be paid each month, so I kept focused on the end result of starting my new role in the bank. I kept a photo of Kieron on my computer, and this provided a constant reminder of why I was working so hard and why it would all be worth it.

Prior to working in the bank branch for the first time, I had to attend two weeks of intensive training which involved commuting to London every day. Following this, I had to attend a residential training course where I had more exams to pass. Anyone who failed these or fell below the expected standard wouldn't be allowed to start in the branch.

There was a lot of pressure on me, as I'd already waited six months just to get to this point. The course also meant leaving Kieron with my mum and dad again, which was hard as I missed not being with him. I was so relieved to pass all of my exams and felt so proud on my first day in the bank wearing my uniform. It had been a long time coming, but I had made it.

Unfortunately my hard work, good intentions, and ethics didn't match with the company's values and beliefs. It felt like I had only just got my foot through the door when I was introduced to the endless, unrealistic sales targets. I have no idea where the good old-fashioned customer service had gone.

Selling a product without a genuine need wasn't in my nature. But it seemed they weren't too concerned about the customers' needs; commission took priority, and I started to dread the hourly phone call from my manager. I would be asked what I was going to sell next and how much commission I had made that day. If my target figure wasn't met, there would be lots of questions about why not. If I didn't have a customer booked in, I was expected to walk around the banking hall until I found one, take them into my office, and make a sale!

Selling was just a small part of the on-going stress; the vast amount of paperwork that accompanied the role was crazy. The compliance rules were so strict that if I made a mistake in my recommendation of products, I could receive a disciplinary warning, or – worse still – lose my job. I liked to take my time over the paperwork to ensure it was all correct, but I was told that I needed to have as many back-to-back appointments as possible; paperwork wasn't seen as a valuable use of my time.

I was arriving at work early, rarely had a lunch break, and then I would leave work late. It wasn't unusual for Kieron to be the first child to be left at nursery and the last child to be collected. This really pulled on my heart strings, but having worked so hard to get my job I felt I had no choice but to carry on. Within six months, I was covering five different branches in the area – and I was exhausted.

Once again, it felt like no matter how much I gave it was never good enough. I started dreading going to work, I began hating conducting a mortgage interview, and I felt an enormous sense of relief if a customer cancelled their appointment. I knew that this wasn't how my role was meant to be; I had hoped for so much more. Slowly I could feel myself feeling really down. It got to the point where I was waking up in the night in tears, I was constantly having nightmares, and often cried on my way to work. I couldn't enjoy the time off I had with Kieron, as my head was always somewhere else. I hated the fact that I couldn't switch off. No matter how hard I tried, my head was spinning and I didn't know how to make it stop.

What was I going to do? I had worked so hard to pass all of my exams, endured six months of temporary work, and then completed all the bank's exams on top of that. Maybe I just wasn't cut out for this job. I spoke to my manager and explained how bad things had been, and asked for some help and support. I was hopeful about the outcome, but we ended up having a heated discussion that ended with her telling me if I couldn't cope with this role there would be nothing else suitable for me in the bank so I should seriously consider my options.

It felt so frustrating, because I knew I was good at my job. I had always received fantastic feedback from the customers, and whenever a manager had sat in on one of my interviews they had always been impressed with how well I worked. The bank's unrealistic sales targets were so much higher than anything I had anticipated. I was working so hard but it was never enough. I had tried for a year to meet their expectations, but I didn't have anything left to give.

A few days after my 'chat' with my manager, I became really ill. I was in bed and found it hard to move without being in agonising pain. Instead of concentrating on getting better, I was still worrying about my workload, knowing the huge pile of paperwork I would be returning to. But my illness literally stopped me in my tracks. I had been pushed to my limits and I knew I couldn't carry on like this. My body was telling me enough was enough.

It was time to choose between my qualifications or my health. My head was in a complete mess. What would everyone think of me if I quit? Did that mean I'd failed again? What job would I go to? But I trusted my instincts and, for the second time, I handed in my notice with no job to go to.

Chapter 5

Quitting a career that I had worked towards for so long wasn't an easy choice, but I decided to seek the work-life balance I had so desperately craved since Kieron was a baby. I wanted to have a good job, to set an example to Kieron, and show him that you can work hard and achieve your goals even if obstacles are thrown in your way. I had tried my hardest but I just couldn't see a way to carry on in the bank role without being carried off by the men in white coats. And that wasn't an option!

Searching through one of the job papers, I saw a vacancy for a part-time cleaner at a local hotel. I had never worked part-time before and the salary was very low, but with the huge saving I would make on nursery fees and the support of Working Families Tax Credits, I worked out I could afford to apply. Working part-time and spending more time with Kieron would be like a dream come true. The slight challenge I had was that I had absolutely no experience for the role, other than cleaning my own house. It seemed ironic that I had worked so hard to gain my mortgage qualifications but now I was seriously wondering if I had enough experience to clean toilets! I laughed to myself as I thought, "Well, if I'm going to be a cleaner, I may as well clean posh toilets!" I submitted my application and hoped for the best.

I can vividly remember driving into the hotel car park for my interview. The confident and composed young woman who had applied for the job was nowhere to be seen. I felt completely overwhelmed and wondered what on earth I'd been thinking the day I had sent in my application. The hotel was lit up and looked very grand from the outside; like somewhere posh people came to for weekend breaks away. I felt out of my depth. My confidence and self-esteem had been knocked as a result of the relentless emotional battering I'd taken working at the bank, and it was starting to show.

Was it too late for me to turn around and go home? I had visions of all these professional cleaners turning up, wearing blue tabards, boasting years' worth of experience and references. There was me relying on the fact that I was a quick learner and that I could tell the difference between a can of furniture polish and a bottle of bleach! I felt like I wasn't good enough for the job and that I was going to make a fool of myself, but took a deep breath and walked in.

As I sat down for my interview, the head of Human Resources looked at me, looked down at my application, then looked back up and asked, "What are you doing here, Cassie?" I took a deep breath and asked if she had children. Thankfully, she did. I said, "Ok, great, let me explain!" I told her briefly about how I had worked full time since having Kieron and how the stress and pressure at the bank had made me completely re-assess my priorities. I explained that I now wanted to spend quality time with Kieron, to release the constant pressure in my mind, and that working part-time could help me to fulfil the work-life balance I wanted.

I don't think I had ever been so nervous while I waited to hear her response. I wanted that job so badly. I couldn't face working for another financial institution, although thankfully my qualifications were on sheets of paper so I would always have them if I ever decided the time was right to go back.

To my relief, I was offered the job – and I couldn't wait to start. Turning up for work in jogging bottoms, a T-shirt, and trainers, was a whole new experience for me but I loved it. I swear I was the happiest cleaner in the world! Plenty of people thought that I had lost my mind. They questioned if I was doing the right thing, but it was my life and I had decided to do what was right for me and my son.

I felt like I had a new lease of life. I loved chatting to the members of the hotel spa, and got along well with my new colleagues. I particularly enjoyed the fact that when I walked out of the door at the end of my shift, no worries or stress came home with me.

I remember vacuuming the spa corridor one day when the manager walked past and asked how I was getting on. I asked apprehensively if I was doing an okay job, as I had no idea what the previous cleaner had been like and hoped they thought my work was satisfactory. He reassured me I was doing a great job and revealed that a lot of the members had commented they had seen a positive difference in the cleanliness. It might sound crazy but I took a real sense of pride in my work.

Although it was far from my ideal job, it was perfect for what I wanted in my life at that point in time. Unfortunately, not everyone saw it from this perspective. One day I was scrubbing the showers like my life depended on it, and sweating like a pig! One of the members asked in a very condescending tone, "Excuse me, dear, do you find your job degrading?" I stood up, looked her straight in the eyes, smiled, and replied, "No. Do you?"

She was a bit flustered, had no response, and walked off for her afternoon swim, muttering to herself. I initially felt angry; how dare she judge me? Part of me wanted to justify myself to her. I wanted to tell her I had a good education behind me and that I had chosen to work as a cleaner so that I could be a better mum. But the anger quickly faded, and I returned to my scrubbing with a smile on my face. I was so much happier than being stuck in the rat race at the bank, and other people's bad attitudes weren't going to change that.

The longer I worked at the hotel, the more involved I became with other duties. I was shown how to give a tour of the gym and pool facilities to potential new members, who were looking to join. I had often watched as people timidly opened the spa door and almost apologetically walked across the wooden floor to ask if they could have a look around. I could completely relate to that feeling of being intimidated; my memory of pulling up into the car park when I first applied for my job never left me.

I soon learned that being my friendly, chatty self was the best way to help these prospective members to feel at ease as I took them around the health club. Some of them had never set foot inside a gym before, and were apprehensive to even walk around. I liked that I could put them at ease, and make them realise they were welcome and that those initial feelings were completely normal.

You would have thought that working there would give me immunity to these insecurities, but I was no different. I loved the idea of working out in the gym or going for a swim after I'd finished work, but something held me back. It was three months before I plucked up enough courage to have a workout in the gym, and six months before I went for a swim in the pool!

Although my body image had improved, this was a big step out of my comfort zone. It seems silly looking back, but I had envisaged the walk from the changing rooms to the pool as being never-ending, and that people would stop what they were doing and stare. In reality, no-one cared. They were there minding their own business, and me and my body weren't on their radar.

Working part-time freed up so much more space in my mind, and I decided I wanted to learn some new skills. A lot of people have heard of Reiki but aren't exactly sure what it entails. I was no different when I turned up for my first treatment. I had been told how a treatment could be beneficial if you were feeling stressed and needed to relax, so that was all the information I needed! I booked myself in for a session, and was looking forward to some much needed chill-out time.

I lay on the massage couch and listened to the relaxing music, when all of a sudden I could feel this amazing warmth over my head. I had to open my eyes slightly to check there wasn't a candle there, but no, it was just the practitioner's hands. I felt very relaxed, but what surprised me more than anything else was when tears began to run down my face. Was that me? Was there something in my eyes? I didn't feel sad or emotional, but they were definitely my tears and there was nothing in my eyes.

At the end of the treatment, the lady said to me, "I'm not here to analyse anything, but it appears there was a lot of emotional pain that you needed to release today." I was a bit confused but I explained that I had been through a lot of pain in the past, although I had moved on now and felt happier. She explained that sometimes we physically move on, but perhaps until then I hadn't released the emotional pain.

I was fascinated. How on earth did my body decide to release that emotion? I felt extremely calm, like a weight had lifted, and my head was clearer. I went back for a few more treatments and gradually realised that when I looked back on events from my past I could now see them in a new light. I could talk about what I had experienced without a heavy pain in my heart or a lump in my throat.

Curious to learn more about Reiki, I decided to buy a book and, by the time I had finished reading it, I knew that I wanted to train and become a Reiki therapist. I never had any intention of starting a business. I just thought it would be an amazing way to help myself and my family.

I also decided to enrol at college for an evening course in counselling, which was something I had been interested in for a while. I really enjoyed meeting new people at college and learning about a new topic. The course also helped me deal with a lot of emotions that I didn't realise were hidden away, as we often had to talk about real-life scenarios.

When I completed my second course, I decided not to study for the final counselling diploma which I would have needed to become a counsellor. Although I found it a very interesting subject, a lot of the time it involved talking about issues from the past and exploring feelings and emotions, but I didn't feel it was really encouraging the client to move forwards. I was concerned that some people could almost become reliant upon their counsellor, instead of feeling empowered to move forwards. I do appreciate that counselling helps a lot of people, especially when they are grieving, but it didn't feel right for me to pursue it any further.

Chapter 6

During the five years I worked at the hotel, I was very content in my personal life. I got engaged, got married, and fell pregnant with my second son. I was so happy to be having another child and was thrilled that Kieron was going to become a big brother. By the end of my pregnancy I had put on three stones, and once again attracted the unwanted attention and intrusive questions about my ever-expanding body. People thought it would be fun this time to jokingly call me "Fatty", but I'm afraid I didn't find very funny.

Do people not realise how vulnerable you feel when you are pregnant? I knew the end result would be worth it, and had no concerns this time about going through labour. At least I had an idea of what to expect; it might be better, it might be worse, but I kept an open mind and prayed that I would be able to have another water birth. I couldn't imagine giving birth on a bed!

I experienced several false alarms, with contractions that kept starting and stopping. So when I was five days overdue and actually went into labour at about 9am, I wasn't convinced it was the real event. Once again I paced the house and had numerous baths, but by 5pm I knew it was time to head to the labour ward, again leaving my bags in the car... just in case.

As I walked into the labour ward the contractions were getting really strong, so I leant forward and waited for the pain to pass. The health care assistant introduced herself and asked if I was in pain. I must have given her a strange look as I muttered, "Yes, I'm hoping I'm in labour." She quickly replied, "Oh right, well I better get the midwife! You seem so calm that I thought you were the other lady who was coming in to have her baby monitored."

The midwife came to see me and made polite chit-chat, but by this point I couldn't sit down as it was too painful. I told her I really hoped I was in labour as it was hurting... a lot. To her surprise – and my amazement – she informed me that I should be meeting my baby in the next hour!

When I told her my bags were still in the car, the midwife then went into a panic, told me to wait on the bed, and said under no circumstances to push. She said she would get the birthing pool ready but we needed to hurry as we didn't have much time. In my head I was thinking, "Chill out, it's fine... don't worry, I won't be having this baby until I'm in the birthing pool!" I was sure there would be a few hours to go, as babies always seem to take longer than expected.

It was like *déjà vu* as I walked up what seemed like the never-ending corridor, then again remembering the amazing relief of the water in the pool. There was no time for bobbing about with a cup of water this time; twenty minutes later Lennie was born. I was a little shocked that it all happened so quickly, but again I experienced that immense rush of unconditional love, emotion, and relief that it was all over.

Bringing Lennie home was pretty emotional. Seeing Kieron's face light up with joy as he cuddled his baby brother for the first time was such a special moment, and one I'll never forget.

I went back to work part-time at the hotel when Lennie was nine months old. It was challenging having one child at school and another at nursery, trying to juggle the school holidays, Christmas plays, sports days, and going to school assemblies. It used to take me an hour to get to work and an hour to get home, due to a combination of dropping the boys off where they needed to be or collecting them, and bad rush hour traffic. It was stressful at times, but I just got on with it. I wasn't working for the money as I was only earning the minimum wage, but I was keen to continue working and felt fortunate that I was able to do part-time hours.

One of the good friends I made while working at the hotel was a personal trainer called Matt. He was extremely hard-working and ambitious, but at the same time very down-to-earth, and we would always have a good laugh.

One evening I got a call at home to say that Matt had been admitted to hospital with bad chest pains, and that doctors thought it might be something serious. I was worried but, as

Matt was the fittest and healthiest guy I knew, I told myself he would be okay and back putting his clients through their paces in the gym again soon.

I got into work the next day to receive a devastating text that the doctors suspected Matt had cancer. My head was spinning. There had to be a mistake; he couldn't have cancer. After some further tests it was confirmed that Matt was suffering from Non-Hodgkin's Lymphoma. Everyone at work was in complete shock.

Any little problems or worries I may have been dealing with just faded into insignificance; I would have done anything to take the pain away from Matt and his family, but I felt so helpless. He was advised that he would definitely have to endure a course of chemotherapy, and there was a strong possibility that radiotherapy would follow.

I have nothing against conventional treatments, but I couldn't stop one thought from going around in my mind. I knew that Reiki could help to keep Matt's mind relaxed as he went through his treatment. I was under no illusion that it would replace the hospital treatment, but I knew people often used Reiki to complement conventional treatment.

Have you ever sat and written a text, deleted it, then rewritten it over and over as you torment yourself about whether to send it or not? That was me. I knew I had to at least offer to help, but I just couldn't find the right words. Eventually I hit the "Send" button, shut my eyes, and hoped the message came across with my best intentions.

I can't tell you how happy and relieved I was to receive Matt's response saying he would love to try some Reiki. He told me he was ready to put up a fight and was willing to try anything.

The day Matt came for his first Reiki treatment was one I'll never forget. His mum and fiancée, Jodie, came and waited, and it was all very emotional. Matt was in a lot of pain and found it difficult to lie down on the Reiki bed. I'm not sure how I found the strength to hold it together, but somehow I managed to get through the treatment and Matt's mum and Jodie both saw what a difference it was making in keeping Matt relaxed.

I asked if they, too, would like a complimentary Reiki treatment; I felt it was the least I could do. They each felt so much benefit from it, and knew how much I enjoyed giving the treatment, that they asked me separately why I wasn't offering Reiki as a business. I gave them the normal excuse people use when they're not taking themselves seriously, and answered something to do with being a busy mum, and working in the hotel, and not really having the time.

On Matt's next visit, he told me he had been offered a complimentary hypnotherapy treatment by a local cancer charity, and that they had also offered him some Reiki. I was like a dog with a bone! Which charity? Where were they based? Did they need any more practitioners? What qualifications did you need? What insurance did you need? Could I volunteer?

It was like something just switched inside me. Having seen how much it had benefitted Matt and his family, how could I not offer to help other people who were going through such an awful time? Matt gave me one of the managers' details and I called her the next day. I was completely honest and told her I didn't have a vast amount of experience, but explained about the treatments I had given to Matt and his family. She was really impressed and said that if I had completed treatments for one of my good friends, then I sounded like an ideal person to volunteer. We set up a meeting so that I could find out more.

One month later I began volunteering at Integrated Cancer Therapies. My first shift was a real mix of emotions. I was feeling so proud that I was going to be helping people who really needed it, but I was concerned whether I would be able to cope emotionally. I would be building up trust, rapport, and relationships with the clients, and I knew there would be some challenging times ahead.

I absolutely loved volunteering. The clients I met were so positive and so grateful for the support from the charity. They all knew that the hospital was doing its job in providing the clinical side of dealing with their illness, but it could be a very rushed environment due to the workload of the staff. To be able to come somewhere where they felt like they could relax and be themselves was invaluable. Chatting and laughter could always be heard from those waiting, or anyone who just wanted to drop in for a chat and some company. When the clients were receiving a treatment, they were full of gratitude; they knew we were always there to listen if they wanted to talk. It was a very humbling experience that really made me feel so grateful for everything that I had in my life.

Matt had come to the end of a gruelling course of eight chemotherapy sessions, and was waiting for news of whether his radiotherapy treatment would be starting before or after Christmas. One evening I had a missed call from Matt and I panicked, hoping everything was okay. When I called back, Jodie answered the phone and told me she had some amazing news. The hospital had just called them to say Matt's cancer had completely gone! There was no scar tissue remaining, and no further treatment of radiotherapy was needed; he was officially in remission.

Tears of relief, disbelief, and happiness followed. I couldn't believe the nightmare had finally ended for Matt and his family. In December, Matt will have been in remission for four years. He has since got married, had his first daughter, and continues to live with such a positive outlook on life.

***

Working at the hotel unfortunately came to an end sooner than I had expected. I was called into a meeting with all of my colleagues and told that our department was being restructured; we would no longer have our current job roles. If we wanted to re-apply for our jobs we could, but the hours of working had now been changed and there was no flexibility. Instead of working from 9.15am-5.15pm Thursday and Friday, the new hours I had been offered were 6am-2pm or 2pm-10pm and would involve working any day from Monday through to Sunday.

There was no way I could fit my childcare around those hours. I wasn't prepared to see my children less, and paying someone to look after them for additional hours whilst I earned the minimum wage wasn't going to happen. I had always worked extra shifts if staff levels were low, and been prepared to go above and beyond my role since I had started. But it all counted for nothing; I was made redundant. I was really upset and didn't feel ready to leave.

It's hard to explain the huge sense of loss that comes with a redundancy. I wasn't losing a job that I had studied for years to qualify in, and it was far from highly paid, but I was losing a job that was perfect for me and which fitted around my family. I appealed the decision, but after becoming extremely run-down and increasingly stressed, I knew it wasn't meant to be.

In the past my manager had told me that they hadn't expected me to last for the first month when I first started. They thought that as I was overqualified for the job, I would probably decide that cleaning wasn't for me. In fact, it was nearly five years later that I walked out of the hotel for the last time. I had no idea what the future held.

Chapter 7

A s I had always worked, I didn't want to stop now – especially when leaving hadn't been my decision.

Matt was telling me that he was working alongside a health and nutrition network marketing company and was seeing amazing results with his personal training clients. I had used some of the company's products myself, and was so impressed with the difference in how I looked and felt that I decided to take a big leap into the unknown.

There was an opportunity to work under the umbrella of this international company, recommending and selling their products. I would also be able to build and train my own team. I knew the products were amazing, but I had no idea if I had it in me to make this work. I decided that I had nothing to lose by going along to the company's training to learn as much as I could – and quickly realised that the support the company offered was phenomenal.

I worked really hard to learn as much as I could and attended many training days; I loved meeting like-minded, positive people. My confidence and personal development soared. I always seemed to have a new motivational book to read, or a new inspirational CD to listen to, which helped to keep me focused.

I had really enjoyed my job at the hotel, but this new opportunity made me realise that I had almost become stagnant from repeating the same duties day in, day out, for almost five years. Working part-time with set hours at the hotel had meant no opportunity for me to progress any further, but now the ball was in my court. My confidence in the products, the company, and finally myself, grew as I found myself having to jump out of my comfort zone on a regular basis.

A friend introduced me to networking meetings, where local businesspeople met as a way of building a referral network. I decided to go along to see if it could help to grow my business, but I found it so daunting standing up and speaking in a room full of experienced businessmen and women. I felt like a vulnerable rabbit in the headlights. I would arrive at the meeting, pick a seat at the back of the room, hide by the buffet, speak when I was spoken to, and then escape as soon as the meeting was over! I was completely out of my depth.

One evening, a lady who ran her own Neuro-Linguistic Programming (NLP) business asked me if I would like to do a therapy swap. We agreed that I could have a free NLP session with her if she could have a free Reiki treatment with me. A week later we met up and she asked me what I would like to improve. I explained how I felt really inadequate and out of place at the networking meetings, so she got to work on changing my thoughts on how I saw myself – and it was really powerful. I was amazed at how changing my thoughts so quickly made an impact on how I felt about myself.

At the next meeting, I arrived early, I dressed in a smart business dress (I had turned up dressed like a secretary for the last few meetings!), I found a chair right at the front of the room and walked up to anyone I hadn't spoken to before, introduced myself, and asked them about their business. It felt amazing! And to my surprise, everyone was really nice, very polite, and extremely interested in my business. I felt like I had turned a corner and began to take myself seriously.

I committed to attending the network marketing business meetings and training, and got to know a lot of the other distributors with the company. I can't tell you how proud I was when I was first invited to speak at our local business meeting, which had about thirty attendees.

As my business continued to grow, I was asked to run a group training session for twenty people. It was all completely new to me, but I embraced the opportunity, spoke about my experience, and was delighted to get amazing feedback. I was then asked to speak several times at our regional training days, which over one hundred people attended. It was after these meetings that I received a phone call I'll never forget.

It was a Saturday morning when my phone rang from an unknown number. I was shocked to hear the voice of one of the top distributors in the company asking if I would like to speak at the national training day, when over 1000 people would attend. The voice inside my head was saying, "Oh my goodness, Cassie, you must be crazy!" But the words that came out of my mouth were, "I'd love to!"

I hung up the phone still in shock. Could I do this? Could I hold it together? I had never had any public speaking training but just kept grabbing opportunities when they came up, and I loved the feeling that I got from speaking. I had received so much positive feedback from my previous talks, but this was taking everything to a whole new level. The Managing Director of the company would be there, along with the top distributors, listening to little old me! I was determined that I was going to do this and I was going to give it my all.

They say if you fail to prepare, you prepare to fail. So I wasn't going to allow that to happen. I wrote out my talk and I practised it over and over again. I visualised myself walking across the stage as my name was being introduced, then I saw myself calmly beginning to speak... well, that was the plan! I began to look forward to the day, although my heart raced every time I remembered what I had committed to. I wasn't going to let my nerves stop me, though; there was no way I was going to let this amazing opportunity slip through my fingers.

Going from a cleaner to presenting to over one thousand people was anything but a natural career progression. But I felt so focused, and my inner drive and determination was in full force. I didn't want to admit it, but deep down I couldn't shake an underlying feeling that I didn't deserve to be presenting on that stage.

At previous national training days, I had sat in awe of the inspiring speakers, most of whom had been with the company for years and had achieved so much. In my case, it was still very early days. I was training a small team and had steady retail sales, but I certainly wasn't a high flyer. Was the audience going to take any notice of me? Were they going to wonder why I'd been asked to speak? Would they see my talk as a great excuse to leave the room and get into the coffee queue early? These were just a few of the niggling thoughts that polluted my brain as I tried really hard to remain positive.

As the doubts crept in, I needed to take action. Whatever happened when I was on the stage, I wanted to know that I had done my best. So I got in touch with a lady who provides a therapy called Mind Detox. It's a powerful technique that can quickly change beliefs that have been instilled in you which aren't necessarily true, but which you believe and live by. I did some research and was encouraged to read it could have powerful results by increasing self-worth and self-belief. This was just what I needed, so off I went!

I explained about my upcoming talk and how I wanted to be the best that I could be. Louise Jensen, my practitioner, listened very carefully then asked me some questions. Before I knew it, tears were streaming down my face. The main belief which emerged was that I didn't think I was good enough; I didn't feel I deserved to be on that stage. It makes me feel sad to remember that experience now. But what I love about Mind Detox is that as soon as the belief has been identified, it can be changed, and it empowers you to move on. An hour-and-a-half later, I left feeling emotionally drained but with a renewed energy and a voice in my head telling me I could do this. I felt ready.

On the morning of my talk, I woke up expecting to have knots and butterflies in my stomach, but I felt fine. I got ready and set off on my drive to the venue; I felt fine. I took my seat in the audience and listened to the speakers who were on before me, waiting for my nerves to kick in, but I still felt fine.

There were two other ladies who were speaking before me. As we were introduced to the audience, we walked across the stage and sat down on our stools. I looked out to the audience and that's when reality hit. I could see rows and rows of people, bright lights, and expectant faces eagerly waiting to hear what we had to say. I anxiously waited for my turn, trying not have a heart attack or fall off my stool! I took some deep breaths in an attempt to remain calm but my body wasn't listening.

Gripping my cue cards tightly, I willed myself to remember the words that I had practised so many times. My head felt fuzzy, my mouth was dry, and I was seriously questioning if any words were going to come out when I opened my mouth. I was about to find out. My name was introduced, and I heard a huge applause from the audience as I walked across the stage to the lectern. I placed my cue cards down, took a deep breath, and looked out into the glare of the bright lights.

I recounted the true story of a chance meeting I'd had with an old friend who asked where I was working and showed an interest in the health supplements. He knew someone who had recently opened a gym and asked if I'd like to meet the owner. My friend thought they could benefit from the products and would happily set up a meeting for me.

Unbeknown to me, this wasn't a normal gym. It was a mixed Martial Arts gym, where they specialised in cage fighting and stick fighting! It may have occurred to you that these aren't the kind of sports that I would participate in, and you would be right!

Although I had worked in a gym in a hotel for five years, I had absolutely no fitness experience (unless cleaning sweat off the treadmills counts!) but that didn't faze me. I knew the products would be a perfect match for the members of the gym. I had been on the supplement training course numerous times, knew the products inside out, and was always ready for a challenge.

Twenty-four hours later, I was getting ready to leave my house to visit the gym when it dawned on me just how far out of my comfort zone this could take me. But it was too late to turn back now.

I met the manager, who asked me to go upstairs and meet one of the instructors. As I walked up the stairs, I heard lots of shouting and it became apparent that they were in the middle of a class. (The men fighting with big sticks in their hands gave this away!)

The instructor introduced himself, kicked his shoes off, and sat on the gym mats. I was wearing a business dress and heels but thought I would follow suit, so kicked off my shoes and sat down, too. He was really impressed with the products and said the class was going to have a short break, so did I want to give a talk to the guys? They all gathered round and asked questions and sampled the products. It went so well that I was invited to go visit another one of their clubs. Two days later I was watching another cage fighter training session, and giving a talk to another group of fighters.

As I shared my story about how you should be ready to jump out of your comfort zone, let go of the outcome, and grab new opportunities, I realised that I hadn't looked down at my notes once! As soon as I had placed my feet where I was going to stand on the stage, something had taken over. I had been clear, calm, and composed. I couldn't believe that I had done it. When I finished and walked back across the stage to another massive round of applause, I got a huge rush of adrenaline. What an amazing feeling! I loved it, and wanted to do it again.

I lost count of the number of people who came and spoke to me after my presentation. They kept telling me how I had inspired them, not only with my story but having the courage to speak in front of so many people. I didn't stop smiling all day. I felt drained and exhausted as I returned home, but I had done it. I felt so proud of what I had achieved.

I should have felt motivated; I should have been fired up, ready to take this positive energy with me as I returned to work on growing my business. For the first time in years, I felt like I had started to find myself again. My confidence was growing, and I was so happy that I had finally found a purpose with my work.

But there was no spring in my step. I was like a swan who appeared to be effortlessly gliding along in life, yet underneath I was frantically paddling. I had been hiding an awful secret and I knew I couldn't carry on like this any longer.

Chapter 8

From the outside looking in, the normal happy and positive Cassie went about her life. Nobody knew I was holding my life together by a thread. Nobody knew about the daily battle that was going on in my head, as I carried on with life the best I could. I continued to try and be the best mum I could be. I would take my boys to school, to meet up with their friends, and tuck them in bed at night pretending everything was okay. I would continue to attend meetings and training events as I pushed my business forward.

But my heart would sink as I listened to the compliments of how well I was doing and how proud I must be with the commitment and dedication I had shown to building a better life for my family. When I met up with my friends, I deflected the conversation away from anything that related to me and my personal life. I dreaded any questions about how I was. If anyone asked why I seemed tired or quieter than normal, I would tell them that Lennie wasn't sleeping properly and I had been up through the night. This was partly true, but it wasn't the whole story.

There were times when I desperately wanted to break my silence and scream that I wasn't okay, that I wanted help. I wanted to crawl under my duvet and cry, and only come back out when everything was okay. I could wish my pain away until the cows came home, but it wasn't going to happen. There was only one person who could make the agonising decision that had left me as a prisoner in my own mind.

Barely a minute went by when I wasn't tormented by my dark thoughts. I didn't know if I was coming or going, I honestly have no idea how I kept up the calm pretence of behaving like everything was normal. Inside, I could feel myself sinking lower and lower. I had forgotten what it felt like to have a clear mind. I was losing focus on my business, starting to withdraw from attending social events, and often found myself aimlessly staring into space searching for answers that couldn't be found.

No doubt it would have been much easier to keep quiet and play happy families; it would only be me that was hurting, and nobody else needed to know. That scenario had crossed my mind, but as time went on I knew I had to be true to myself.

I wanted someone to tell me this wasn't real and that everything would be okay. Could life really be this cruel? I didn't want to admit to myself, let alone to anyone else, that I had found out six months earlier the devastating news that history had repeated itself. I had tried, but I couldn't accept what had happened. In April 2012, I made the heartbreaking decision to end my marriage.

It would be impossible to describe in words the sheer devastation that followed in the hours, days, and weeks that followed. Knowing that my world was about to collapse for the second time was simply unbearable. I was convinced that someone was having a serious laugh, at my expense. I had no idea how I was going to carry on looking after my boys and how I wasn't going to fall apart. My head was constantly spinning. It pounded as I desperately asked the questions: Why me? What's wrong with me? What am I going to tell the boys? Where are we going to live? How can I find the words to tell my family?

I put off phoning my mum and dad for as long as I could – for two reasons. The first reason was that I know, as a parent, that all you ever want is for your children to be happy. I seemed to be doing a very good job of failing at that! They had seen first-hand how awful it was the first time my world collapsed, and had been elated when I'd found happiness again. They had absolutely no idea that anything was going to change this, and I knew how devastated they would be, not only for me but for the boys to lose their stability, too.

The second reason was that my sister, Sam, who lives in New Zealand, was pregnant with her second child. My mum and dad had spoken about the possibility of going to visit her over Christmas to meet their new grandchild. They had asked me how I would feel if they went to New Zealand for Christmas. Like most families, we always spend time together on Christmas Day, but I had enjoyed being with them for the past few years and knew what it would mean for them to be with Sam and her family, living so far away. I told my parents to go ahead; we would miss them, but it was more important for them to go to New Zealand. They were a little reluctant but booked their tickets, innocently assuming that I was still happily married.

A few days after I knew they had paid for their tickets, I sat quietly in the garden trying to pluck up the courage to tell them my news. I was pretty sure they would not have booked to go if they had any idea that I was going to be on my own for Christmas. I'm typing this now in tears, recalling that awful phone call; it was like déjà vu.

Once again, I'm not sure what I said (this kind of crap really ought to come with a handbook). I listened to their shock, disbelief, and devastation; they couldn't believe what had happened. My dad shot back to reality. "Oh no, Cassie, I'm so sorry, but we've already booked our tickets to see Sam at Christmas." I admitted that I had held off telling them I had ended my marriage, as I'd wanted to make sure they were going to New Zealand. I didn't tell them that I had already begun to dread Chirstmas, as I had no idea what I was going to do. But that was the least of my worries.

I felt like I had failed Kieron and my parents for the second time. I felt such a failure, and started to question everything. The house I had lived in for twelve years and fought so hard to keep would now have to be sold. I was going to be a single mum again; I would now have two children to two different dads. I kept hoping and praying that I was going to wake up soon and it would all be a dreadful nightmare. Surely this couldn't really be happening!

Years before, I had sat and sobbed by Kieron's cot, telling him how sorry I was that I had split up with his dad. He had just been a baby, and that had been hard enough. Kieron was now nine, Lennie was three. How was I going to tell Kieron that for the second time in his life his family was splitting up? How was I going to tell Lennie that he wasn't going to be living with his dad now? My heart physically hurt with pain at the thought of the conversation and the boys' reaction. They were so close and loved spending time together, but they would be spending less time together now when they were each away with their dads.

On a normal day when I called the boys downstairs it was to tell them their dinner was ready, or to ask them which park they wanted to go to. Today wasn't a normal day. This time I was calling them downstairs to tell them that all our lives were going to experience big changes. I just had to hope that I didn't end up sobbing again, like the first time around.

Their reaction wasn't at all what I had expected. Kieron asked if he would still live with me. He then explained to his little brother that he would now visit his dad at weekends, just like Kieron did. They were both very calm. Then Kieron asked if he could go back to his room and continue playing his game, and Lennie carried on watching his TV programme! I felt really proud of how well they had dealt with it.

The boys took everything in their stride. They have always maintained regular contact and have a very good relationship with their dads.

I decided that night that I could no longer carry on with the network marketing business. My motivation to succeed was my family, but this had disappeared along with my hopes and dreams of working towards a better future. How could I train a team, pretending to be confident and happy, when in reality I was a complete mess and could barely string a sentence together without crying?

The thought of losing my house and potentially my business scared me to death, but what really haunted me was spiralling back down that deep, dark road of self-hatred and destruction that I thought I had left in the past. I could still clearly see the image of that scared girl standing in the changing rooms, wearing a pair of size 8 jeans, convinced that she was fat, ugly and worthless. That vulnerable girl who didn't think she was good enough could so easily come back to haunt me at any given moment.

I was petrified of self-destructing. I knew how easy it would be to lose myself again, as my self-esteem had already started to slip away. The constant negative thoughts that were flying through my mind were in conflict with a feeling that I had deep down.

I didn't dare look too far into the future, but something kept telling me that I was going to be okay. There was a tiny spark inside me that wouldn't go out, and I wasn't going to fight it. I had two children to look after and there was no way I was going to let them down; I would always be there for them, no matter what happened. Somehow I had to keep myself sane.

I'm not sure how I coped with getting through each day, but I dug really deep and decided that I wasn't going to give up on the business. More than ever, I wanted to set a good example to my boys and keep going.

It wasn't easy putting on a brave face, but I took each day as it came. One important lesson that I learned from going through a very stressful time is that you soon learn who the genuine people in your life are. The turmoil can quickly separate your true friends from those just interested in finding out about any gossip, and others who fade away.

I was devastated when I heard some rumours that were going around about why people thought I had ended my marriage. I had made the decision not to tell everyone what had happened; frankly, it wasn't any of their business. I had enough on my plate without being inundated with endless questions when I didn't know the answers myself.

One afternoon I was telling one of my friends how upset I was about these rumours. Her reply was, "Are these people going to cry at your funeral, Cassie?" I looked up and smiled. We had both listened to the same motivational CD that explains the importance of keeping true and genuine people around you, and not worrying about what the others say. So if you are ever faced with a situation like I was, ask yourself, "Will these people cry at my funeral?" Chances are, they won't even be there. It was a very good reality check – onwards and upwards.

I booked myself onto a one day mind-set and motivation course to help push my business forward. I wasn't sure if it would help, as I still felt very low, but I knew I would really benefit from some training in remaining positive. The trainer, Dave O'Connor, captivated me from the start. I was genuinely intrigued, and at the end of a truly inspiring day I decided to pay good money to work with him on a one-to-one basis in his individual coaching programme. If you have ever been in a situation when you've felt that you can't afford to do something but you know that you actually can't afford not to, then you'll understand. I owed it to myself to give this my all. Maybe this could be the missing link I needed to keep going.

I told Dave in our first consultation that this course was make-or-break for me. No pressure then! The mind-set coaching I had signed up for was to help me maintain and grow my existing network marketing business. Dave would ask me about the goals I wanted to achieve, how I wanted to see myself, and how I'd feel when I achieved them. He would then make me a powerful, personalised MP3 recording which I would listen to twice a day until our next coaching session. I had completed a lot of self-development work over the previous year, but combining coaching with my personal recordings took everything to another level. I was stunned with the results.

I could have easily been forgiven for declaring that life was too hard, unfair, and that quitting was the easiest option. Instead, I started to feel calmer, in control, and I had more confidence in myself than ever. I pushed forward, continuing to attend training courses, and recruiting new team members. And I was amazed that this new-found confidence began to ripple through every area of my life. Instead of setting off my self-destruct button, I began to look after myself. I was happy with the person I was becoming, and knew that punishing myself with food wasn't the answer.

And, thank goodness, the girl who hated her reflection the first time her world collapsed, has never re-emerged.

My self-esteem and my business were parts of my life I could control, and I was so happy that I was able to keep them. Unfortunately, the same couldn't be said for my house.

Chapter 9

Moving house is an extremely stressful event at the best of times. When most people choose to move, they are doing so as a family to a bigger house or to a better area – and they still almost crack up in the process!

I felt angry and upset, because I didn't want to move house. I had lived there for 12 years and, having managed to keep my house the first time my world collapsed, it felt even more painful having to sell it now. Feeling sorry for myself wasn't going to put a roof over our heads, though. I reluctantly started looking for a new house to rent.

I had never rented before, but how hard could it be? I began to look at properties online and became scared that we wouldn't be able to find a house. There was certain criteria that pretty much every house had:

- They were reluctant to rent to anyone receiving housing benefit.
- They were reluctant to rent to anyone who was recently self-employed.
- They were reluctant to rent to anyone who owned a dog.

When I called a few estate agents, I was greeted by an enthusiastic member of staff but they soon realised that I fell into all three categories and politely ended the conversation, saying that they couldn't help me. What on earth was I going to do? I stared out the window in a daze; it was pouring with rain. When was this nightmare going to end? As I stood there looking out, the rain stopped abruptly, the sun came out, and a beautiful rainbow appeared. Was this a sign that things would be okay?

I wasn't convinced, but it gave me some renewed hope to start my search again so I sent a group email to all of the estate agents in my town. When I checked my phone later, I had a missed call from an unknown number. I felt a glimmer of hope as I called it back and discovered it was a landlady who had a house in the area I was looking for, and wondered if I'd like to view it.

Then I heard the dreaded words, "I just need to check that you don't have a dog." My heart sank. I replied that I did and was about to thank her for her time, when I heard something that I really wasn't expecting. She told me that she had been very impressed with how professional my answerphone message sounded when she'd called, and that she had a good feeling about me. She was willing to meet up when we viewed the house, and discuss the possibility of allowing my dog.

I could have cried with relief as I hung up. Someone was willing to give me a chance! I had been told so many times that you don't get a second chance to make a good first impression, and this was living proof. It turned out the house was perfect. I paid an extra deposit for my dog and began to pack up the house I was reluctant to leave.

Preparing to move from the house which I had lived in for so long was both physically and emotionally draining. The night before the removal men came I didn't finish packing until 1am, and was completely shattered by the time I fell into bed.

I tried to switch off my mind, which had decided that replaying the memories of the last twelve years would be a good idea. I remembered when I had brought both of the boys home from the hospital as babies. There had been so many happy times in the house, but there was a small part of me which felt relieved to be closing the door and leaving the bad memories behind.

When my alarm clock woke me, I didn't have any time for nostalgia. It wasn't even 8.30am and I was surprised my hair hadn't turned completely grey. Lennie was too ill to attend nursery, so he would be with me for the day. My bed couldn't be taken to pieces so it was stuck in my bedroom, and the dishwasher hadn't been collected as promised. But my main concern was that I still hadn't received a call from my solicitor to say that the house sale had gone through! They had been promising the exchange was going to happen for the last four days, but there had been last minute complications which meant I had no option other than to exchange and complete on the same day, which is far from ideal.

I called my mum and dad in the hope that they could come and help look after Lennie and my dog, and thankfully they drove over as quickly as they could. I contacted a local furniture removal company and asked if they could come round in the next hour and help me break up my old bed; in return, they could have my dishwasher for free! They agreed.

The removal men arrived and, bit by bit, my house was emptied. Everything was packed and ready to go, but I still hadn't received a call to say that we had exchanged contracts. The removal men were on a tight schedule and insisted we didn't have any time to wait around, so I had to leave.

I walked round the house one more time, stepped out of the front door with tears in my eyes, then locked the door. I had committed to paying for a six month rental contract, but I still legally owned my house and was committed to pay the mortgage payments for the foreseeable future until the contracts were exchanged. I had no idea what would happen if the sale fell through at the last minute; there was no way I could afford both payments. I had no choice but to leave my old house, trusting that everything would be alright.

I had driven halfway to the new house when my phone began to ring. My heart was racing as I pulled over, stopped, and answered. I didn't hear much of what the solicitor said other than the words, "We're about to exchange the legal contracts and we will call you back once we have completed." What a relief! It was finally happening, the sale was going through. I arrived at my new house, pulled up on the drive, and my phone rang again. The solicitor confirmed everything had been completed, the sale had gone through. It was only four weeks since I had accepted the offer on my old house and everything had happened so quickly. One door had closed as another one had opened, literally!

I went to bed that night exhausted. Well, I say bed, but I actually slept on the floor for the first two weeks as the mattress I had chosen wasn't in stock. I had contemplated whether I should wait for the one I really wanted to be ordered, or to settle for another mattress that I wasn't so keen on. The guy who worked in the shop helped me decide when he said, "Think about it this way, you're possibly going to sleep on this every night for the next five years, some things are worth waiting for!"

He was right, and it is as true in life as it is for mattress purchases! That night I fell fast asleep wrapped up in a duvet on the floor, feeling proud that I had survived the move (with only a few new grey hairs!).

I was up early the next day to take the boys to nursery and school as normal. I then headed off for a day of meetings in Northampton, before driving to Milton Keynes for another meeting that didn't finish until 9pm. A lady I spoke to there couldn't believe I had only moved house the day before; she thought I had lost the plot! But I had made a commitment to meet people, so that's what I did. I love the saying that if you want something badly enough, you'll find a way – and if you don't, you'll find an excuse. It was business as normal from then on.

Having the business to focus on was really good for me. The training that I had with Dave had made a huge difference, and not only in my business; it influenced every area of my life. I had made a commitment to myself not to crumble, and I wasn't going to look back now. I embraced the coaching, enjoyed going out more, and I wasn't the only one who noticed. Friends would come to visit my new house, half expecting to find me rocking in the corner, feeling sorry for myself, and slugging from a bottle of vodka! Instead, they found a very calm, happy Cassie, with a spring in her step and a new outlook on life!

This wasn't to say that I took ending my marriage lightly – far from it. I was devastated that it had come to that, it hurt more than words on this page could ever describe. However, I was still young (well, that's what I told myself!), I still had my life ahead of me, and I wasn't going to spend it living in the past, wallowing in self-pity. There was only one person that could move me forward, and that was me.

I came to the end of my coaching sessions with Dave but committed to carry on listening to my recordings on a regular basis over the next few months. It was at the end of the summer when I was aware that something was starting to change with how I felt about the business – and I didn't like it. I have no idea what happened. It was a very slow and subtle change that made me question if network marketing was right for me. Bit by bit I realised that I wasn't feeling as motivated as I had been.

I carried on regardless and put it down to not being in a routine, due to the school holidays. I had booked to go to a huge motivational training day at the start of September, and I couldn't wait to attend. There's nothing like being surrounded by one thousand committed, motivated people and hearing inspiring speakers, to give you a kick up the bum and get you back on track.

My mum and dad came over early to babysit and I set off with some of my team members. There was always a buzz of excitement at these events, and I was looking forward to a big dose of positivity. But as we sat and listened to the different speakers, I was aware that I didn't feel very comfortable there. I tried to focus on the next person speaking but the feeling wasn't going away. I was surrounded by people, yet I felt so alone. I didn't feel inspired, I didn't feel motivated, and I certainly didn't feel like I wanted to be there. I just wanted to go home.

Driving back, I was giving myself a good talking to (in my head, as I was driving a car full of people!). I kept telling myself, "What on earth are you playing at, Cassie? You need to snap out of this and get focused again. You have just been through the most stressful time of your life but you've got through it. It's not time to start losing your focus now. You need to find your motivation quickly, pick yourself up, get a grip, and carry on."

If only it was that simple! I tried so hard. I dug deep, stepped up my activity, read another motivational book, listened to my recordings from Dave... but it just wasn't happening. I couldn't fight the feeling that network marketing just didn't feel right any more.

It still feels stupid even writing it now. "I'm going to wind down a business that I've worked so hard to build, because it doesn't feel right!" How pathetic does that sound? But it was the truth, and that's what I did. I just couldn't find it in me to keep going and I was scared.

It had been ten years since I'd had Kieron, and I had carried on working all of that time. I had now worked full time, part-time, and even tried network marketing. Stopping work was never going to be an option. I was still determined to set a good example to my children; I wanted to make them proud of me. At that moment in time, that was looking highly unlikely.

Chapter 10

Something no-one tells you when you have children is how hard it is to go back to work after they're born. People will judge you if you do, they judge you if you don't. Trying to achieve a work-life balance seemed like an impossible task. I felt like I was literally banging my head against a brick wall.

Unanswered questions were spinning around in my mind: "What on earth am I going to do now? How can I work but still be there for my children? Do you not think I've dealt with enough crap already? I'm willing to learn whatever this lesson is, but will someone please give me a clue? Can someone help me to find out the next step forward... anyone ?"

At times in my life when I feel like I am on a slippery slope, I have to say I am definitely getting better at asking for help. I was talking to a friend and explaining how lost I felt and that I had no idea what I was going to do with my life. She said if I was open-minded and wanted to try something different, then she knew a lady who may be able to help. I took Sandie's number and decided I wanted to find out more. I wasn't entirely sure how she was going to help me, but I trusted my friend's advice and gave her a call out of desperation.

When I called Sandie, I poured out a summary of what had been going on in my life and how I felt lost with no direction. I explained that I didn't want to give up, but at the same time I wasn't sure for how much longer I could be strong. I told her about my network marketing business and how my motivation had disappeared overnight, leaving me feeling confused, angry, and frustrated with myself.

Having someone truly listen to you is such an understated and powerful tool, and that is exactly what she did. Sandie listened to everything, took it all in, and cast no judgments over my past. She gave me some really sound advice, but what came out of her mouth next left me speechless. She told me that there was a reason it had never worked out when I'd worked for other people, as it was time for me to do this on my own.

There was a confused silence, then I asked her to repeat what she'd said. It sounded like she was suggesting I should set up my own business! That is exactly what she meant. I remember thinking, "You can't be serious", and laughing! She must have me confused with someone else; I wouldn't have a clue where to start. I had no qualifications other than my GCSEs, a GNVQ, and my mortgage CeMap exams – and I certainly wasn't going to be a self-employed mortgage advisor!

Working with the network marketing company had given me a lot of personal development, but I had been under a very protective umbrella where they told you everything you needed to know. The training, marketing, and pricing was already tried and tested, so I just had to repeat their proven business cycle that had been in place for over 30 years. Setting up a business from scratch would be a huge challenge. It's not uncommon for people with years of qualifications, funding, and experience, to fail.

Sandie wasn't accepting my objections, though, and continued talking to me as if it was a done deal. She told me that I had a natural ability to make other people feel at ease and that I was a lot more inspiring than I realised, so it was time to share this. I was still confused but as I didn't have many other options, I tried to remain open-minded. We spoke in depth about what really motivated me and what I really felt passionate about. I explained that I wanted to help others to move forward with their lives, to share that it is possible to overcome adversity and challenges no matter what life throws at you. I admitted I would love to play a part in this journey in helping others, but saying the words and implementing that in a real life business seemed worlds apart.

Sandie's advice was to go away and give some serious thought to the personal lessons I had learned through my own experiences, and how they could be used to help others. I felt a bit more positive about the situation, even though I still doubted where this was going. My life to date had been just that, my life; it was fairly normal to me, because I had lived it day-in and day-out. But I began to realise that other people didn't see my life as normal. They often said that going through everything I had, and coming out the other end with a positive outlook on life and refusing to quit, was really inspiring. I still wasn't completely convinced, but I sat down that night and started to write about my journey so far.

I had only written two pages when I had to stop; I couldn't see my computer screen through the tears. What was I doing? I had done so well moving on, and now I was dragging all of these memories back up again. How on earth was that going to help?

I put my doubts to one side, wiped my tears away, and carried on with what I had set out to do. When I got to the end, I felt a sense of relief. As I read back over my notes, something became apparent: I hadn't self-destructed when my life broke down for the second time.

I hadn't realized how badly my confidence had been affected from gaining weight with my children and then drastically losing weight when I had split up with Kieron's dad. I had hated myself and punished my body when my world collapsed for the first time. So why didn't that happen again the second time? Surely it should have been a lot worse? I had lost so much more the second time, so why didn't I lose myself?

As I continued to read over my words, everything started to make sense. The coaching with Dave had played a huge part in keeping my head in the right place. It had enabled me to focus on remaining positive, and drowned out the negativity surrounding me. Strengthening my mind-set had made me realise that I didn't need to punish myself for what had happened in my life. My body wasn't perfect, but I had accepted myself for who I was. And this had played a huge part in the difference between make-or-break. That night, I went to bed feeling drained. I still had no idea where this was going, but I felt better for making a start.

***

Two weeks later, an idea came to me while I was driving. Could I make similar MP3 recordings to the ones that Dave had made for me? Instead of them being used as a business tool, I could work with women to help them feel genuinely good about themselves from the inside out. Could the recordings help them to feel stronger, and build internal walls of confidence to help stop them from self-destructing? By visualizing how they wanted to see themselves, could they feel happier and take back their control by combining this with a consistent healthy lifestyle? So many women are trying to be everything to everyone that they can easily lose themselves along the way.

Many women are brainwashed by the rose-tinted illusion that weight loss equals happiness, but I knew this wasn't true. I'd had firsthand experience of how it's irrelevant what you look like if you don't feel good about yourself. If I could help others to regain that control and ultimately help to increase their confidence and how they felt about themselves, that would be amazing. It would also enable them to make changes to their lifestyle and break any unwanted habits.

The more I thought about the idea, the more I believed it had potential to work. Particularly with weight loss, it can be so challenging to stay motivated long enough to see positive results, and that's often why people give up. Sadly, this failure can leave you feeling low so you console yourself with wine, crisps, and maybe a few donuts! You then have to psyche yourself up ready to start the process again! Thousands of women are on this relentless cycle, which is knocking their self-esteem and confidence even lower. If they have big decisions to make in their life, perhaps with work or relationships, they can feel like they are not good enough and inferior. They feel drained and exhausted from living their life in fear, whilst putting on a brave face to the outside world. I had been there. Maybe, just maybe, I could help them.

I sent an email to Dave explaining what had happened. I told him he might think I had gone slightly mad, but that I had decided not to carry on with the network marketing business. I wanted to help people in a similar way to how he had helped me, but working with women on a personal level with wellness and confidence. I was really encouraged when Dave replied that he thought that would work really well and encouraged me to go for it.

To find out if there was a demand for my business idea, I booked some meetings with a couple of personal trainers and a weight loss consultant I knew. I explained to them what my idea was, and how I had potentially come up with a solution to help keep their clients focused and motivated in between their training sessions. This could help to increase their clients' results, satisfaction and retention. It was a way of providing clients with support when the personal trainers/consultant weren't with them.

Most clients who attend personal training sessions are fired up and motivated while they are training. But that might only be for up to three hours a week, so what happens in the other 165 hours? For example, the food choices they make between the sessions are so important. Even if the clients do see positive results, that alone isn't necessarily going to help them to feel good about themselves. They also need to change their mindset.

It was a big step to share my idea, but the trainers' response was really positive. I asked if they would be willing to give me some clients I could work with on a trial basis, in return for testimonials which I could use to promote my business.

Within a matter of days, I had the names and phone numbers of several women who were willing to work with me. I felt scared, apprehensive, and excited as I picked up the phone for the first time. These people had never met me before, but they were willing to hear what I had to say. As soon as I introduced myself and explained how I wanted to help them, it was like their barriers dropped. I was able to build up rapport really quickly, and asked some questions until I had enough information to make their individual recording. They had no idea if my recording was going to help them but they trusted me, which was a huge step in the right direction.

I was excited as I got to work making the recordings. I emailed them across with instructions to listen twice a day for a week, then I would get back in touch to see how they were getting on.

I absolutely loved making the recordings; even though it was all so new, it felt so right. I found it came naturally to put myself in each woman's shoes and to see their goals through their eyes.

Two weeks passed, and the testimonials started to come in. The results shocked the personal trainers, they shocked my clients – and I have to admit, they really shocked me! All of the ladies had seen really powerful changes in their life-styles, felt a huge surge of motivation, and some long-standing habits had already been broken. One lady told me I had changed her life!

I had to make sure I was sitting on my own each time I received another email containing the feedback, as it became inevitable that I would start to cry! I felt so happy and proud that the trials had worked. I knew then that I owed it to myself to take "me" seriously and have the courage to run with this. I began to tell people what I was doing, and made enquiries about getting my website set up. It still felt a bit surreal, as I wasn't sure where it was all going; I didn't even have an idea what I was going to call my business! But it didn't matter. I had gained a new sense of momentum and I wasn't going to stop now.

Chapter 11

It felt so good to have a goal and something I could work towards, but I couldn't ignore the cold dark winter nights that had set in. Mum and Dad left to fly to New Zealand in October; I wouldn't see them again until February 2013. They had been so supportive over the last few months, always helping with the boys whenever they could. They are my only family living close by and, although they knew I had friends that I could turn to if need be, we were all aware it was a long time to be apart. It was sad to say goodbye.

I was dreading Christmas. The cheesy adverts had begun, there were happy families and happy couples everywhere, promoting what a special time of year this should be. It seemed like a constant reminder of everything that I wouldn't have this year. I tried to keep myself busy and focus on the business, but when the boys weren't with me I felt sad and lonely. Money was tight so I couldn't justify going to spend the weekend with friends or taking myself out for the day. Some friends said they would come round and visit, but they were often busy with their own plans or would cancel.

The last thing I wanted to do was to have a job, but I longed for that social engagement with people; I missed not attending a work Christmas party. Sometimes, when the boys were with their dads, I could spend four days on my own without seeing or speaking to anyone. Some people would comment that I was lucky to have a lay-in and all that time to myself, but I didn't feel very lucky. I hadn't chosen to have children to not see them. I missed them when they were away and hated how quiet the house was without them.

I felt strongly that I didn't want to just see my boys for half of the day on Christmas Day. I had done that before when Kieron was younger, and I hated it. It doesn't matter which half of the day you have, it's not the same not being with your children. To avoid that, I decided I would have my Christmas Day with the boys on Christmas Eve.

Quite a lot of people thought I had gone mad when they asked how I was spending Christmas. They would ask why I wasn't going to be with my children on Christmas Day, or why I was letting their dads be with them all day when I was going to be on my own. If you've read this far, you'll know that when I feel strongly about something that involves my family, I'm not concerned with what others think. No-one else is living my life. I'm not always right, but I make the best decisions I can on what I feel is right.

I told the boys that we would write to Santa and ask him to drop the presents here before he flew to New Zealand to start his rounds there. They were thrilled at the idea of having two Christmas Days. I also said they could choose to have whatever they wanted to eat for breakfast, lunch, and dinner that day, and that they could play at home for the entire day as we wouldn't be going anywhere. They were pleased about that, too.

All I needed to do now was to decide what I was going to do on the real Christmas Day without them. I had heard about people working for homeless charities at Christmas and thought what a lovely selfless act that was. About a week later I saw a post on my friend's Facebook page saying that he was going to be working for a homeless charity in London. Intrigued to find out more, I looked on their website and read they were looking for volunteers to work in the temporary centres set up over the Christmas period to make a difference to homeless people.

Until then, I had always thought that volunteers would be handing out soup and blankets before sending the homeless on their way. What I discovered was that they offer so much more; they were appealing for doctors, dentists, opticians, chiropodists, to give up their time for free to offer these invaluable services which homeless people may not otherwise be able to access. They were also looking for complementary therapists to provide some much needed relaxation.

When I'd moved house to live on my own with the boys, something had to give and unfortunately it had been volunteering my time at the cancer charity. I had really missed working there, so this would be a way of me giving something back. My life was far from perfect but at least I had a roof over my head, food to eat, and my family. I decided to apply.

On the application form they stated that the hardest shifts for them to fill were Christmas Day and Boxing Day, because there was no public transport into London. I was free on those two days and decided that if my application was successful, I would drive myself into central London on both days to be there. This was the girl who used to be frightened of driving, scared stiff of driving in the dark, and petrified of driving on motorways! For years I avoided driving in the dark and on motorways at all costs, but when I was working in network marketing I had no choice because meetings were spread out across the country. So, slowly but surely, I had begun to drive up and down the country. My confidence had definitely increased, but committing to driving into central London was a whole new ball game.

My decision was made, though. If I was selected, I would overcome my fears and drive there. I submitted my application and hoped for the best. A week later I was thrilled to receive the confirmation that I had been accepted.

In the run-up to Christmas I threw myself into preparing to launch my business, and before I knew it our Christmas Eve had arrived. I had booked for me and the boys to go to our local pantomime as a treat. It was a bittersweet experience as the boys loved it, but everywhere I turned were happy families; another reminder of what I'd lost. When we arrived home, I got the boys into bed and brought their presents downstairs to be wrapped. I was overcome with emotion as I sat and sobbed over the wrapping paper. My reaction took me completely by surprise, but I just let the tears flow. I had no regrets about the decision I had made, but I had never imagined spending Christmas on my own with the boys. We would definitely make the most of it.

As it turned out, we had a fantastic day together. I hear of so many people who run around like headless chickens at Christmas. They try and please everyone, visit people who don't bother with them for the rest of the year, and then feel exhausted and stressed out. We stayed in our pyjamas most of the day, and enjoyed eating bacon rolls for breakfast, pizza for lunch, and pancakes for tea! The boys loved staying at home and playing with their toys until they got collected by their dads at 7pm.

I can't deny it felt strange after the boys had left, but I just pretended it was a normal day as I prepared my packed lunch for the following day. There would be no Christmas dinner for me this year. The charity had advised us to bring high energy snacks and drinks, as we might not get a chance to stop for a proper break. I went to bed early wondering what the morning would bring.

I woke up early on Christmas Day; the house was too quiet. I kept thinking of the boys, but just reminded myself we had already had our Christmas Day. I have no idea what possessed me to log onto my Facebook account before I left. My newsfeed on a normal day can get on my nerves with the sometimes exaggerated "Everything is so perfect in my life" posts. As expected, they were everywhere that morning.

People couldn't wait to share "My children have opened their huge mountain of presents", "I can't wait to see my amazing family", "This is the best Christmas ever" – and it was only 7am!

I am aware I may sound like a complete Scrooge but when you have spent Christmas Day without your close family and your children, it does make you spare a thought for others who are alone or missing family members. It can be an extremely difficult day and a very sad time of the year.

One Facebook post which caught my eye certainly wasn't a happy one. A guy who was volunteering at the same homeless centre as me was devastated that his motorbike had broken down near Luton. He was really upset and apologizing that for the first time in years he wasn't going to make it to volunteer, as there was no other transport available. I thought how upset I would be if my car had broken down that morning; it's not like you can tag along to someone else's Christmas Day. It would be awful to sit on your own all day with no plans.

Without thinking twice, I replied to his post saying I would be passing Luton in an hour and would be happy to pick him up! I'm not stupid, I know it's not in the "Health and Safety" etiquette to drive to a random guy's house and drive them into central London! But sometimes you just have to trust your instincts. It was Christmas Day and I wanted to help.

I pulled up in his street and called him to say I was the girl outside in the silver car, as I realised we didn't know what each other looked like! We chatted and laughed all the way into London and, as he had volunteered before, he knew exactly where to go and exactly where to park, which was a huge relief. When we walked in, I suddenly felt apprehensive. It was meant to be a happy day but how would all the homeless people be feeling? Could I hold it together and keep a lid on my emotions?

I had no idea what to expect as I made my way to register and was shown to the room where I would be working. I will never forget my time there; it was an experience that is so difficult to put into words. There were hundreds of volunteers, all working together as a big team, which created an amazing atmosphere. I was humbled by the attitude of the homeless people, they couldn't thank me enough for giving up my time and they all loved their Reiki treatments. I asked them if they could remember the last time they had closed their eyes and relaxed – none of them could.

It was an emotionally draining day, but I wouldn't have changed a moment of it – and it certainly made me so grateful for everything in my life.

Chapter 12

When Christmas and New Year had passed, I felt a huge sense of relief. I had got through an awful year and was really looking forward to what 2013 would bring. Unfortunately, the momentum that I had gathered before Christmas was nowhere to be seen; I was having big doubts about starting up on my own.

As I drove home from a meeting on the 10th January, 2013, I decided it was time to launch my business. I hadn't planned to do it so soon; my website still wasn't ready; I wasn't ready. But I knew these doubts weren't going away, so I needed to take action quickly.

I can vividly remember typing onto my new Facebook page "Cassie Farren – Body Confidence Trainer" then pressed the button to make my business page live. People set up Facebook pages every day, but this was different. I felt scared and anxious. Was I about to completely humiliate myself?

I had an unwavering determination to help women who felt lost, alone, and frustrated. I knew that I could help to empower them to take control back, to build their confidence from the inside out, and to truly feel good about themselves. The fact was, other than that, I didn't feel like I had anything else going for me. I had never been to university; I had gone from becoming a mortgage advisor, to a cleaner, and then tried networking marketing. I was taking the risk of setting up my business in the middle of a recession, and working around my two young children. I had no experience in setting up a company, and had just built my business on the foundations of my personal experience, with a job title that I had made up! Who was going to take me seriously?

The next morning, I woke to an incredible response:

- I had *over one hundred* "Likes" on my Facebook page
- I had been asked to speak at a networking event
- I had been asked to write an article in a magazine
- I had received an enquiry from New Zealand
- and I had a message from a lady who wanted to book a consultation with me for THAT DAY!

By that afternoon, the consultation was completed. I sent her recording, and less than 24 hours after launching, the money from my first sale was in my bank account! It was such a surreal moment, I remember thinking to myself, "This works! This actually works!" I couldn't believe the amount of support I had received from people wishing me luck and telling me how they could resonate with my message. I was so happy that I hadn't allowed my fears and doubts to take over, and I had a renewed belief that I would make this happen.

When I introduce myself as a Body Confidence Trainer, I can be met with what I have affectionately called "The Look" – the one when someone quickly looks me up and down and then has a slightly confused look on their face. You can almost hear them thinking, "What would she know? How could she relate to women who are self-destructing, feeling lost and afraid, and slowly losing control while putting on a front for the outside world to see?"

I am well aware that I no longer come across as a woman who hates herself and her body, or has low self-esteem and confidence issues. So how can I relate to other women who may want to work with me? A guy at a networking event asked me, "Do your clients want to work with someone who is slim, happy, and confident?" He wasn't being rude, he was just being honest. The answer is "Yes, they do." But I've learned that it definitely helps once they know about my own personal journey, as this builds up trust and rapport. They know I won't judge them and I understand how they feel.

Do I help people to feel good naked? That's one of the questions that I am often asked. I have also been asked (seriously!) if there is any undressing as part of my Body Confidence workshops. (No, there isn't!) People hear the words "Body Confidence" and think that I am a glorified weight loss consultant. They assume that my role is to help women lose weight and "Ta-da", they will be super happy and confident. It doesn't work like that.

I have to confess that I didn't know what to call myself when I started my business. I knew the ladies I would work with MIGHT want to lose weight, but the priority was to help them to feel happy and confident in their own skin.

- I knew that they would be feeling out of control.
- I knew that they would feel like, somewhere along the way, part of them had gone missing.
- I knew they may be feeling annoyed at themselves after many soul-destroying "diets".
- I knew they may be afraid of change.
- I knew they felt they owed it to themselves to try something different before they sank any lower.
- I knew they would be feeling stuck.
- I knew that decisions they had once made calmly and with conviction could now feel daunting, as though their voice didn't matter.
- I knew they might feel people may have taken advantage of them, leaving them feeling low and emotionally fragile.
- It could be affecting their work; it could be affecting their personal relationships.
- They'd feel frustrated, as though they should know better.

You know you deserve better.

I specialise in helping women to have the courage to

move forward with their lives. This may involve breaking the chain of emotional and comfort eating, which can play a big part in decreasing your confidence. This may involve incorporating new habits you would like to see in your life, perhaps increasing your exercise, or having some more time for yourself. This may involve seeing yourself as someone who is worthy, who is valued, and who is good enough.

There may be an important event coming up in your life where you want to turn up with your head held high and feel like the best possible version of you. Once your inner belief and your self-confidence is reignited, it will empower you to become unstuck and allow you to gain momentum.

If you are happy and confident on the inside, you do not need to seek that external validation that can lead to many insecurities and unwanted habits. You will be back in control, ready to look forward to the future again. You will be on your journey to be the best possible authentic you

That is Body Confidence.

I firmly believe that you need to be able to control your emotions to put an end to this vicious cycle. If you strengthen your mindset so that you can perceive yourself as someone who is worthy, and finally feel you are good enough, you can make the right choices with food. Then weight loss will occur, almost as a side effect. Food has become such an integral part of our lives and we can substitute almost any emotion or any situation with it. We eat when we are sad, tired, fed up, bored or lonely. We eat when we are happy, to treat ourselves for "being good", and to celebrate almost any event (including going to the gym!).

There are not many women who have never turned to food to comfort themselves. We are conditioned as children to reward ourselves with food, and when our emotions get out of control this behavior can be reverted to and can be very challenging to stop. Food is often used to preoccupy our minds temporarily, to help to forget about our emotions.

A lot of women don't see this as being a problem. After all, it's not like they're turning to class A drugs. Instead, they are turning to the enticing aisles in the supermarket, which are accessible 24 hours a day. I'm not a qualified dietician but I have spoken to enough women to know that there aren't many long-lasting, sustainable ways to lose weight. It can be extremely difficult to stay motivated long enough to see results. More often than not, women fall off the wagon and then comfort themselves with more food, beat themselves up for failing again, get angry as they feel they should know better, and then psyche themselves up to start over again! If they do see results and reach their goal, it is a common trait to fall back into old habits and gradually put the weight back on – and sometimes more on top.

Many of the women I have worked with have been facing a silent battle alone. They often feel like they have failed, that they should know better, and ultimately that they are not good enough. Many have been through a messy separation or a divorce, where they have been emotionally battered, leaving them feeling even more miserable and less in control.

They all have one thing in common: they have had enough.

They know deep down that they deserve more. They want food to play a smaller part in their life. They often feel scared and apprehensive as they nervously tell me they have tried everything and they are ready to try something new. They are filled with hope as I explain just how powerful our thoughts are, and that there isn't much education on this. They will have tried nearly every way to change their eating and exercise habits, but it's unlikely they have ever taken time to refocus and strengthen their mind-set.

I work with women who are ready to take back their control once and for all. It is completely client-led; they all know what they want to achieve, and they all know the steps they need to take to make progress. The challenging part for them is consistency. It is the easiest thing in the world to set a goal. To actually carry out daily habits to achieve this, day-in, day-out, is why people want to work with me. It gives them hope, a kick start, and lasting motivation.

I do not need to know a detailed history of their lives, but I do need to know that they are committed and are ready to take themselves seriously. When I have a consultation – either through Skype or on the phone – I will ask them about their lifestyle and in which areas they want to make changes. This can include making healthier choices with food, reducing the amount of alcohol they drink, feeling motivated to take more exercise, ensuring they get enough sleep, making sure they have some quality "me time", or they may want to have more time with their family.

Once I have enough information, I will then write out

"Their story" and read back over my notes. I then sit quietly, close my eyes, and put myself in their shoes, before I plan out how they will begin to make the changes they want to see in themselves and their lives.

If they have an event coming up like a holiday, a wedding, a family party, or a special meal (it can be any day where they want to look and feel their best), I will incorporate a visualisation into their recording. I have made recordings for ladies who want to feel more confident in their work – it may be a promotion they want to go for, or an important meeting where they want to walk in with their head held high and owning their space.

The recording will help to reinstall that confidence and self-belief that can get trampled on, often as a result of a negative relationship that has left them feeling that they are not good enough. I ask my clients to go into detail about the special event, about what they would like to wear, how their hair will be, where the event will be, who else is going to be there, and how they want to feel on that day. One of the reasons my recordings are so powerful is because they are so personalised. I make the recordings to relaxing background music, and I pride myself on making them as "real" as possible.

When I first started my business, I researched other relaxation recordings that can be found and I was shocked when I often wanted to turn them off after about 30 seconds. I consider myself to be very open to alternative therapies but there were lots of people with droning, monotone voices that were asking you to "Count backwards from 20 as you sit under your special tree", or "Take yourself to your special place as you hear the water lapping against your feet and the cool breeze in your hair!" That does nothing for me, and it's no wonder some people find it hard to relax or commit to listening to them on a regular basis.

The ladies I work with look forward to listening to their recordings, they have even said that they sleep a lot better and wake up feeling refreshed. There are not many of my clients who haven't cried (happy tears!) when they first listen. It is normally the first time they have heard something so powerful, that is tailor-made to reignite their belief in themselves, and teach them it is possible to get back on track and finally begin to love life. Once I have finished a consultation, I can already hear a change in the client's voice. I have given them hope, and they know they have made a really positive step to get back on track to living the life they deserve.

My bespoke recordings are never any longer than five minutes, and the client commits to listen to this twice a day. If they cannot find ten minutes a day to making positive changes to their life, then I will be honest and say they are not ready to work with me. And that is okay. I'm not going anywhere, and will be happy to work with them whenever they are ready.

I commit a lot of energy into each recording, and I treat every woman as though they are the first client I have ever worked with. I want them to get the best possible result, which is why it is important that they listen on a regular basis. The more powerful part of their mind (the subconscious) will begin to absorb the information on their recording, and they can start to see changes in as little as two weeks. It starts with changing their thoughts, which leads to a change in their actions.

I always make it clear that I do not have a magic wand but I have made a very powerful tool that will work... if they do, too. Women find that they have increased motivation, a calmer mind, they feel valued, worthy, and empowered, and they make better choices – not just with food, but also in their lives. They are amazed that after years of going around in circles, they have finally found something that works. I am often thanked by women for the part I have played in changing their lives, but it is them who have made the changes. I just provide the tools to enable them to finally take back their control and believe in themselves again.

Starting a business could be likened to having a baby. You have time to prepare, you do your research, you think you know what to expect, but in reality nothing can prepare you for the emotional rollercoaster that follows.

The lows in business can be unbearable. I soon realised there would be a lot of these and that they can appear at any moment without a warning. I have lost track of the amount of times I have nearly called it a day. The people close to me have seen the struggle I have faced behind closed doors, along with the tears that have fallen, as I've questioned if I could carry on. I have had unforeseen challenges thrown at me left, right, and centre, and it's been harder than I could ever have imagined. All I ever wanted was to be a good mum to my children, have a happy work/life balance, and to help others; at times it has looked like it wasn't meant to be. Thankfully, whenever I have had challenging times, there has been something that has picked me up and made me decide once again to finish what I have started.

The highs are like nothing you have ever experienced. You feel invincible and so proud, and know that all your hard work has paid off. It felt amazing when I ran my first Body Confidence workshop. I decided to hold it in a meeting room at the hotel where I used to work. It was like déjà vu as I pulled into the car park, and I had a flashback of the time I had driven into that same car park a few years before, convinced that I wasn't good enough to be their cleaner. Now I was a business owner, about to run a workshop which had sold out!

The feedback I got from that evening was overwhelming. Over the next few months I ran more workshops, took part in radio interviews, I was quoted as a Body Confidence expert in Weight Watchers magazine, and was a finalist in an awards ceremony. I began receiving bookings to give more motivational talks, and started to realise that it was my personal journey behind the business which drew people to work with me. Once they knew about my highs and lows I could build the rapport and trust needed for them to open up to me, then I could help them on their journey. There is nothing you can compare to the feeling of being told that you have helped to change someone's life for the better.

In March 2014, I was very proud to reach the finals in

the Networking Mummies UK Ltd Awards. I was in the "Against All Odds" category, which seemed very fitting. I guess if there were three words to describe me and my business, those would certainly be a perfect match.

This category was open to any business which had overcome adverse circumstances and successfully fought to continue its journey. I was invited to speak to John Griff on BBC Radio Northampton about the awards. I had been a guest on John's show several times and was looking forward to my interview.

As I sat in the studio waiting to speak live on the air, John asked me if I had chosen my dress for the awards ceremony. It just so happened I had been shopping the day before, so I took my phone out of my handbag and showed him a photo I had taken while wearing the dress I had bought. I had taken the quick picture in the changing room and text it to two of my good friends. When the dress quickly got their approval, it was a done deal. That was the outfit I was going to wear.

As we began our interview, John asked me about my business and what had inspired me to help other women. He asked if there had ever been a time when my body confidence had been so low that I couldn't look at myself in the mirror. I answered honestly that I couldn't remember not being able to look in the mirror, but I had certainly hated my refection. I remembered that day when I had been so shocked to be standing in the changing rooms wearing a pair of size 8 jeans, and the realisation that I wasn't fat and ugly.

John pointed out the irony of how just a few years ago I had stood in a changing room hating my reflection, yet I had walked into his studio that afternoon and shared with him a photograph of me in a changing room, proudly wearing a dress to represent a business which I had set up to inspire other women help find themselves and avoid self-destructing. I was momentarily lost for words – not a great idea live on the radio! – but he was right. I felt quite emotional as John congratulated me on my success of coming full circle on my journey, then wished me all the best for my business and the upcoming awards.

Going to the awards ceremony was a completely new experience for me. I didn't win, but it was still a huge honour to have made it to the final. I knew that the judges would be making their decision on each of our personal journeys, and for that reason I didn't feel like we were competing. To have come so far, we were all winners in our own right, and I was proud that not only had I set up my business, but that I was now using my experience to help other women with what I had learned from my journey.

Chapter 13

Earlier this year, after a run of very challenging events, I was given a glimmer of hope. I was told that I qualified to apply for some business funding from the Northamptonshire Enterprise Partnership which, if successful, would give my company a huge boost.

I was really excited about the opportunity until I opened the email and read the extremely long and daunting application process. There was page after page of detailed questions about my plans for the future, including questions like: what staff was I going to employ? What training would I give them to stay motivated? Who were my strategic alliances going to be with? Could I send a detailed spreadsheet with a two-year cash flow forecast?

My heart sank and my eyes filled with tears. I told myself, "I don't think I can do this." I was so proud to have traded for over a year with no prior business experience, but this was scary stuff. I closed the email and missed the deadline for submitting my application.

Thankfully, I received a friendly kick up the bum from someone close to me. I was reminded that of course it wasn't going to be easy. The grant was going to be given to people who were serious about their business and who were prepared to put in the effort to complete all of the paperwork. I decided to call the company and ask if there was someone who could help me with the parts I was stuck on. They were extremely helpful and booked me in to meet an advisor. I was told to complete and email as much of the business plan as I could, and they would discuss it further at my meeting.

I was so nervous driving to the meeting. Would they take me seriously? I knew that I had achieved amazing results with my clients, but my business is very unique and I sometimes wonder if people will "get it".

I needn't have worried. The advisor was extremely complimentary about what I had achieved on my own and, although the process was very competitive, he advised me to apply. With his guidance, I went away and finalised my proposal and cash flow forecast, and submitted it a month later. Whatever the outcome, I had overcome my initial doubts and I felt proud of that.

I was thrilled when I found out I had got through to the final stage. I was invited to a panel interview, where three business advisors would question me about my business and my proposal for the funding. By the time I arrived at the panel meeting, I had completely changed my mind-set from the girl who had experienced doubts a few months back.

I had repeatedly visualised myself walking into the room, having belief in myself and my business. I went in with my head held high and complete faith in what I wanted to achieve. I enjoyed the meeting with the advisors, as I told them with complete composure and confidence about the plans I had for the future of my business. By the time I left, I knew that I had done my best.

Just 24 hours later my hands were shaking as I clicked on the email informing me that I had been successful! I had to read it three times before I could absorb the information. The panel believed in me and they believed in my business! It was such a proud moment knowing I had been awarded the funding which would enable me to take my business to the next level and share my message on a larger scale. I would be using the money to publish my first book, The Girl Who Refused To Quit.

Booking a professional photoshoot was a strange feeling. I used to be one of those women who hated having her photograph taken; the one who either hid behind the camera, or went out of the room whenever a camera was around. As a child, my teeth were very crooked and I wore braces from when I was 12 until I was 20. They were painful, they were ugly, and they did nothing for my confidence or self-esteem. I would reluctantly give half a smile with my mouth closed, and if I laughed I put my hand over my mouth. I had friends, I was happy, but I hated smiling.

Has anyone ever made a derogatory comment to you which still rings in your ears years later? I was 12 years old, and it was a normal school day. I was in an art lesson when one of my friends thought it would be funny to ask a boy in the class if he would go out with me. I hadn't asked her to ask him. In fact, I didn't really like him. But I never forgot his reply...

His answer was, "With those teeth, I would rather drown in a cesspit." At the time I didn't know what a cesspit was, but I did know that it was a pretty harsh insult. (Definition of a cesspit: "A pit which can be used to dispose of urine, faeces, sewage or refuse.") He laughed it off, and to this day I bet he has never thought twice about the comment. But it stayed with me for a long time.

It surprised me that I was now looking forward to having my photograph taken for the front cover and the inside of my book. Donna had only just started taking photos when she told me we had some great images and were finished part one of our photoshoot. She told me I was easy to photograph because I smiled so easily. Smiled so easily?

We then set off to a stunning location to take the photograph which would be used as my front cover. We had planned on arriving just as the sun was going down, and got there just in time, laughing and giggling as we ran to get everything set up. I felt relaxed, content, and completely present in that moment as we captured the beauty of the sun setting.

When Donna sent me through the photographs a few days later, I was stunned. She had captured the moment perfectly! There she was, The Girl Who Refused To Quit, looking calm and serene, accepting what had been and gone, and looking forward to whatever the future held.

I felt as though the last few months had been testing me to see how badly I wanted to continue, and if I was prepared to fight for what I believed in. It would have been so much easier to eliminate the stress and to walk away. But I had refused to do that. I had made a promise to myself that I was going to make my boys proud, and that I would not quit.

The bond I have with my boys gets stronger and stronger as time goes by. They are growing up to be such caring and thoughtful, well balanced young men. I will never take for granted the quality time we spend together, and will always be so proud to be their mum.

I now have the most amazing man in my life, and I have truly never been happier. I would go through everything again in a heartbeat if I was told this was how my story was going to end. But I hope this is just the beginning...

Chapter 14

18 months later...

There is *nothing* that can prepare you for becoming a single mum for the third time.

Once is hard; twice is devastating; three times... well, it just shouldn't happen.

In January 2016, my life collapsed in an instant. One minute I had what appeared to be the perfect life, the next I was sitting in disbelief, trying to figure out what the hell I'd done in my previous life to deserve this utter devastation — again.

I didn't scream and shout. I didn't sob or wail. And I certainly didn't update my social media status to tell the world that I was newly single. I sat quietly staring into space, wondering if I could hold it together whilst I cooked and ate dinner with Kieron before his dad collected him. I would tell him soon, but at that moment it was all too raw. I had no answers to the questions he would have, and I didn't want him to worry over the weekend.

I decided that I would have the awful conversation that no parent should ever have to have (let alone more than once) when the boys were back from their dads'. We ate dinner as normal as I held back the tears, knowing that our lives were going to be very different from now on. I felt that I had failed both of my children, and my parents, again.

There is *nothing* that can prepare you for making that agonising phone call to your parents for the third time to tell them that their daughter and grandsons will be starting life, once again, on their own. It was heart-breaking hearing their voices break with emotion as they also tried to come to terms with the disbelief of what had happened. They wanted to offer me words of comfort, but there were no words that could take away the pain. I felt like the black sheep of the family who had caused them even more upset. Yet I knew they still loved me unconditionally, and that meant the world to me.

I didn't sleep at all that night. Instead, I watched the memories of the last few years pass me by. I was scared by the uncertainty that we faced again of moving house and not knowing where we were going to live. But I had to trust that we would be okay. Strangely, I felt very calm over that weekend, but there was still one more conversation I needed to have that I was dreading.

There is *nothing* that can prepare you to sit your children down, look them in the eye, and tell them that once again their life would never be the same. I believe that children should be exactly that – children. They should not have to be faced with the same hurt, pain, and devastation that can come with being an adult, but unfortunately there was no way I could protect them from this hurt. I told them very honestly what had happened and that I didn't know when or where we would be moving, but I wanted to make sure they knew that I would always be there for them and that I didn't want them to worry about anything.

I am in awe of how resilient and understanding they were, and I believe they handled the situation better than many adults may have done. I could not have been any prouder of them if I tried.

I found myself wondering if I had the strength to carry on with my business. Could I swallow my pride and tell everyone that The Girl Who Refused to Quit had given up on her dreams and had actually quit? The thought left me full of dread, and actually made me feel physically sick. I had worked so hard and wanted nothing more than to keep sharing my message. I wanted to inspire others to follow their heart and believe in themselves, but –without realising it – I had ignored all of my own advice and lost a lot of faith in myself over the last year.

It shocked me that when I had lost so much and now had the perfect excuse to take the easy way out and quit my business, there was absolutely no doubt in my mind that I would find a way to make this work. There was still a tiny spark within me that I could feel growing day by day, telling me that I still had a purpose, I had a message, and that I had come too far now to stop. Others may have lost belief in me, but I had not lost hope or belief in myself. It had wavered, yes, but I had to believe there was still light at the end of what felt like a very long tunnel.

The past year had been a complete roller coaster in my business. I had put so much energy into publishing my book, and was beaming with pride on the day when the first copy was delivered to my house. I remember seeing the delivery van pull into my street, I literally ran to my front door and stood on the driveway with a huge smile on my face to be greeted by a confused delivery man, with a strange look on his face! I explained that he had just delivered the first copy of my book, which turned his confusion into a smile as he told me he actually felt like he'd done something worthwhile in his job.

As he left, I stood with the cardboard box in my hands, shaking. Part of me wanted to rip it open quickly, but part of me was scared. This was it: my moment, my journey, my book – all neatly bubble-wrapped in a box. I slowly opened the package and held the book in my quivering hands. Wow! There she was, The Girl Who Refused to Quit ready to share her journey and hoping to inspire others with her story.

I wasn't naïve enough to think that from then on my life would effortlessly fall into place and I would be able to retire off the royalties. But I had no idea that two weeks later I would be turning up to my own book launch in a lot of pain and feeling like a fraud.

I wholeheartedly agree with the principle that when you get given an opportunity, you should say yes and then find a way. So when I was asked to speak at a motivational event for women in Scotland – and promote my book, of course – the answer was a big yes! It didn't matter that it was going to take me seven hours to drive there, or that I would need to arrange childcare for the whole weekend. It was a fantastic opportunity and I would find a way.

My unwavering determination was put to the test when, 48 hours before I was due to start my journey to Scotland, I was involved in a car accident. Thankfully, it wasn't serious, but it did leave me very shaken up and in a lot of pain with whiplash. But there was no part of me that questioned whether I would still be part of the day. I sorted out the endless insurance phone calls, then booked myself a train ticket that would see me getting on four trains each way, with the combined travel time of about 18 hours.

I was in a lot of discomfort from sitting down for so long, which didn't help, but I used the travel time wisely to practise my talk (in my head!) and chatted away to some lovely people. Being part of the event was an amazing experience, and my talk received some fantastic feedback. Several ladies in the audience spoke to me afterwards, telling me that I had really moved and inspired them, which made it all worthwhile. It's not always easy running your own business, but I'm a firm believer that your goals need to be bigger than your excuses.

I returned from my trip feeling exhausted from all of the travelling, in pain from my back seizing up, and panicking about my upcoming book launch, which was due to happen in a few days. I had reluctantly arranged the launch, after being persuaded that I ought to have one. I didn't really know what all the fuss was about; I didn't feel like I'd done anything that special. I had only written a book!

I invited my close friends and family, who were all really excited about the evening, but I didn't share their excitement. I messaged my friend the night before and asked what actually happens at a book launch, as I had no idea! On the car journey there, I found myself wondering if anyone was going to catch me out, as I'm just me, Cassie; I didn't feel like a real author!

I have to admit I was wrong. It was a fantastic evening, and really overwhelming to see all of my good friends and family who were genuinely all very proud of what I had accomplished. It turned out that I did know how to host a book launch, and I felt like I had actually achieved something by the end of the evening. After many hours of blood, sweat, and a lot of tears, I had done it. I was a very proud (real!) author.

So why was it that over the days and weeks after my launch I began to feel increasingly low in myself and that something was missing? I was thrilled to have been asked to speak on the radio again, only to become very run down and to catch the flu. I very reluctantly had to call the radio station and tell them that as I could hardly speak, I would unfortunately have to cancel.

I was sitting in the car, having just dropped Lennie off at school, when I made the call. When I hung up, I cried and felt so frustrated, then returned home to sleep until it was time to collect my son again. I was still in a lot of pain with my back and was exhausted from waking up every night in a lot of discomfort.

Thankfully, after a few days I started to feel better, but I still couldn't shake off the feeling that something didn't feel right with my business. I got cross with myself, thinking, 'here we go again, you and your stupid feelings of something not feeling right!' I loved working with ladies, helping them overcome low body confidence, but something was telling me that there was more to my business than this. I wished I knew what it was, as my motivation was running low, and so was my bank balance.

When I had first started my business, I'd had no idea how much money I would need to invest to keep everything running. I was fortunate not to have overheads like an office to rent, but my business bills soon added up and if I wasn't earning any money these bills still needed to be paid. I felt like I was constantly juggling money and making tough decisions – should I go to a networking meeting, or should I take the boys swimming? I felt guilty if I invested money in my business and the boys missed out, but then if I didn't push forward and invest in my business I might have to resort to the nightmare of getting a job and leaving the boys with a childminder. I understand that a lot working parents need to do this, and I had been the same until I started my business a few years before.

I loved the flexibility that my business gave me to be there in the school holidays, if the boys were ill, or so that I could attend the school events. And I knew it would be hard to sacrifice this. My time with the boys was already shared with their dads, so putting them into childcare would reduce our time together even further. There were some days when I really wished that someone would give me a job description and monthly salary just to stop the continual money worries and the constant struggle that was going on in my mind.

This battle started again when I saw a lady I knew, Jan Taylor, was offering a new intuitive coaching programme. It was aimed at people who were feeling stuck in their business and knew they needed a change in direction to get them back on track. I read Jan's advert about three times before deciding to go for it. I needed some help, and I needed it fast. I had experienced many ups and downs in my business, but this time I felt like I was sinking and needed a helping hand – maybe even an oxygen tank!

It's difficult when you have built your reputation as (what appears to be) a successful business owner, and then have to admit that you're feeling really down, especially when you've just published a book declaring that you are The Girl Who Refused to Quit. I decided I needed to be completely honest with Jan, so I told her everything. It felt like a relief to share how I was feeling, but I was still very apprehensive about how I would find a way to move forward.

Jan's intuitive guidance proved to be worth its weight in gold. Over the course of the coaching, we established that overcoming low body confidence myself and helping other women with the same problem had been part of my journey, but it was only a small part of my story. It had been two years since I had set up my business, and I had, without realising it, stepped onto a never ending emotional roller-coaster. There were some days when I wanted to shout about my business from the rooftops; there were other days when I wanted the world to swallow me up! I had faced and overcome so many challenges, yet I had still managed to keep going by increasing my resilience, constantly stepping out of my comfort zone and keeping a positive mind-set.

My own experiences had made me passionate about helping other women who had the courage to set up their business, to assist them to have the confidence and belief in themselves and their business, no matter what happened along the way.

Jan and I decided that I didn't need to change the way I worked or the techniques I used, as my bespoke meditations could be just as powerful for empowering women in business. I just needed to change the niche of who I worked with. That sounds pretty simple when I type it out, but at the time it was a big change and it felt daunting.

However, Jan's coaching helped me to have the courage to make all the necessary changes, and I felt confident that this was the right direction I was taking. I also decided to set up a free group on Facebook, which I hoped would empower and support women in business. The online world can feel very busy and crowded, but there had been many times when I had felt stuck and alone. I hoped that by starting my group, 'Empowering Women in Business', it could prevent others from feeling this way.

I felt so grateful to Jan for her help and I proud of myself that, once again, I had dug very deep and found a way to carry on. I was learning the hard way that running your own business can be extremely challenging. It was hard enough setting up the practical elements – website, blog, newsletter, learning social media, copy writing, managing accounts, mastering marketing, sales, and following a business plan – but these all felt relatively easy compared to constantly keeping my head in the right place!

My new clients are women in business who are feeling stuck. They are procrastinating instead of taking action, and losing belief in themselves and their business, instead of gaining momentum. They have started to compare themselves to others, to overthink decisions, and are questioning if they are worthy of success or if they should call it a day. They don't feel good enough and have considered quitting, but there is something inside that won't let them. They know they have a purpose, and through my bespoke meditations I help them to reignite that spark so they fall back in love with their business, and take confident, consistent action to move them closer towards their goals.

I felt so happy that I had found a way forward, but a few months later my business still wasn't progressing financially. I would make money, invest that money in my business, and then repeat! They do say it takes three years to get your business established, but I was already two-and-a-half years in, and I starting to wish the last six months away in the hope that I'd reach the point where I was making a regular income.

One afternoon I was feeling low when I received an e-mail from a lady I'd met when I was giving a talk. In her message she told me how much I had inspired her, and that my talk had really helped her with a challenge she was facing in her life. But it was the subject of the e-mail that caught my eye: 'Do you know any busy mums looking for the perfect part time job?'

I know that she hadn't thought for one minute that I would be looking for a job, but I knew that I couldn't carry on the way I was for much longer. I wrote my reply whilst tears were streaming down my face.

'Thank you for your e-mail and your lovely feedback. My business isn't progressing as I had hoped and I would like to apply for the job.'

I don't know how long my finger hovered over the 'send' button before I pressed it, but I do remember the awful feeling of shame and humiliation as I did. The last time this lady and I had spoken, I had been standing in front of an audience telling everyone in the room how they should never give up, and there I was a few months later on the verge of quitting my business and asking if she'd like me to send across a copy of my CV! There was part of me that didn't want to get a response back, as this meant it was real.

The reply I got made me cry even more. I was really sobbing, with snot and everything! The subject had been changed from 'Do you know any busy mums looking for the perfect part time job?' to 'You are an amazing woman ☺' They always say that the people who know you won't judge you; that day I was reminded of this.

It turned out that some other work came in through my business shortly after we exchanged messages, so I didn't end up applying for that job. But two months later, work had gone quiet again and I found myself reluctantly driving in a daze to an interview.

Just the day before, I had been giving a presentation to a group of local business owners, and received amazing feedback. They told me how I should be so proud of how far I had come. Yet I went home and cried that evening, because I knew it was time to face reality and I was scared that the presentation might be the last talk I ever gave. I know they say that some people fear public speaking more than they fear death, but I have grown to love it. The feeling of connecting with an audience through sharing my journey is indescribable.

The following morning, I reluctantly phoned a local company about a part time position I'd seen advertised. The lady said I sounded perfect and asked if I could drive over immediately for an interview. An hour later, I had been interviewed and offered the job. Receiving a job offer is meant to be a time of joy and celebration, but there were no celebrations happening.

I was feeling really fed up and wondering what was the point? What had been the point of working to help so many other people for the last three years? What was the point in me baring my soul at every talk I gave and on every page of my book, hoping to motivate and inspire others? What was the point of all of my hard work, when three years later I was going to apply for a job and leave all that effort behind?

There was the chance that I could still run my business and have the job, but my life was already very busy with family commitments. Would I be putting too much pressure on myself? Would I be foolish to carry on with my business and pay all of my expenses, if it wasn't generating much income? My head was a mess and my heart was devastated but I booked onto the company's training course, hoping in the meantime for a small miracle.

Chapter 15

Three weeks later, I was driving to my training course. I had tried to stay positive and remind myself that the extra money would be helpful for the family, and the job didn't have to be forever. But I wasn't convincing myself, and the tears that I'd been trying to hold back started to roll down my cheeks. The next few days passed by in a blur. I cried every day in the car on the way there, and found myself staring into space every evening, feeling like a complete failure. I felt so low that everyone who cared about me begged me not to take the job; they could see how unhappy I was. The positive and cheerful Cassie they knew was nowhere to be seen. I told them I didn't want to accept the position, but I knew we needed the money, and my business wasn't making any.

My miracle may not have happened immediately, but shortly after completing the training course, I was due to renew my business insurance. Thankfully, I managed to find a quote for a third of the price I'd previously been paying. I also had some more work come in, which gave me another glimmer of hope.

I decided I had to take a chance and give my business one last push. I just couldn't bring myself to start the job so I thanked the company for the opportunity but didn't accept the position.

It was around the same time that I had the idea of launching an online empowerment programme for women in business. I wondered if I could make an online course, with video modules which clients could work through at their own pace whilst listening daily to a motivational meditation, and I would support them in an online group. I knew from experience which topics most women in business needed support with, and felt confident that I had the answers in my own empowerment toolkit that I had built up over the years.

Maybe, just maybe, this could work. I knew it wouldn't be easy and it would involve a lot of work, but I was determined to give this my all. I had no idea where to start; I had no idea how I would overcome my technical demons to implement the programme; and I certainly had no idea that three weeks later my life would collapse, leaving me staring into space and questioning everything.

To say this was a challenging time would be an understatement. But once I had found a new house for me and the boys, that tiny spark of ambition inside me refused to go out. In fact, it started to glow. I had to believe that I had come this far for a reason, and once I decided to put all of my energy into looking after myself, the boys, and my business, it gave me a lot of hope for the future.

I began working with another coach, Emma Holmes, who runs an amazing course which helps women to launch their business online. I felt so focused as I worked for long hours every day, learning everything that I needed to do to make my dream of an online programme become reality. It wasn't easy. I was emotionally and physically drained from constantly working, packing boxes, and looking after the boys, but I kept on going.

Two days before we moved into our new house, my online programme went live. I cried with happiness when I received a notification to say I had got my first client! I was so proud of myself for committing to help others at a time when I could have been forgiven for giving up on everything and collapsing in a heap on the floor.

I also feel very proud that I have now found the courage to introduce Reiki healing into my business. I know without a shadow of a doubt that receiving regular energy healing has helped to keep my mind calm when it so easily could have broken down. I feel compelled to share this amazing gift with other women in business.

I have surprised myself with the strength I've found over the last few months. I don't look back with any anger, hurt or resentment, instead I choose to look forward with hope for my future. I've only got to listen to the laughter from my boys and see the smiles on their faces to know that we have not just survived, but thrived; we've come through this even stronger as a family.

There is *nothing* that can prepare you for your life collapsing and changing beyond recognition three times, but I truly hope that by sharing my journey I can inspire you to hold your head high and live life on your terms – no matter what crap gets thrown at you along the way.

> *'Sometimes when things are falling apart they may actually be falling into place'*
> *- Unknown*

Cassie x

The Girl Who Refused to Quit

Cassie Farren

Poem by Cassie

Your questions have now been answered,
You know the steps to take.
Don't be afraid, be true to yourself,
Have faith, it's not too late.

It's time to replace your tears with smiles.
The best is yet to come.
You've got this chance to live your life,
Your happiness has now begun.

Follow your heart and follow your dreams,
Have the courage to take the right path.
Believe in yourself, maintain your pride,
You've already come so far.

Hold your head high, live life on your terms.
You can do this, it's time to commit.
Know you're worthy, take one step at a time.

From

The Girl Who Refused To Quit.

Contact Cassie

To find out more about Cassie and her work, please visit:
www.cassiefarren.com
For daily inspiration and updates, visit Cassie's Facebook page:
www.facebook.com/cassie.farren
For media enquiries, please contact
media@cassiefarren.com
For corporate enquiries and motivational speaker bookings, please e-mail
enquiries@cassiefarren.com

Cassie would love you to leave a review for her book on Amazon.

The Elements of

Active Prose

Writing Tips to Make Your Prose Shine

Tahlia Newland

The Elements of Active Prose: Writing Tips to Make Your Prose Shine.

Copyright © 2014 Tahlia Newland. All rights reserved
Published by AIA Publishing

ISBN: 978-0-9942192-2-0

Cover design by Velvet Wings Design.

Edited by Kevin Berry.

"Tahlia Newland has written a concise and valuable guide for authors who want to make their prose dynamic and engaging." Mary Maddox, BA Hons Creative Writing, and recipient of a Writer's Grant and two Literary Awards from the Illinois Arts Council.

"I can definitely recommend this book to authors who are swimming in the void without anything in the way of concrete advice on how to beef up prose. This book is concise, well written, and laid out with reference in mind. It's easy to navigate as well, with clear examples of where many writers get hung up." Brent Meske, Assistant Professor, English at JoongBu University

"The Elements of Active Prose is a concise guide for writers of fiction. The author offers concrete and practical tips for making one's prose style more effective and includes advices on how to work with editors and make productive use of criticism. Beginning writers need the information in this book, and more experienced writers will find valuable pointers about craftsmanship and the benefits of a positive attitude." Dream Beast. Vine Voice

Contents

Foreword

This book is the result of my search for an answer to the question: what makes good prose? I gleaned the information in this book from various places: workshops I attended, courses I undertook, books and blogs I read, and mainstream publishers, authors and editors whom I worked with and talked to. I searched for the answer over a period of five years while I wrote and refined my Diamond Peak Series. Even when the manuscript of the first book, *Lethal Inheritance*, was doing the query rounds of the big publishers with my agent, Debbie Golvan, I continued my study and line edited my book again. I found pearls in a variety of places, but never did I find all the vital information in one place.

When I began writing reviews of both mainstream and indie published books, I discovered that many indie books lacked the quality of prose I saw in mainstream fiction. Though the level of copy editing was adequate in some—and not so adequate in others—few of them had been line edited, hence the problem.

When I began doing manuscript appraisals and, after gaining an editing qualification, offering editing services, I shared the tips I'd learnt with my clients. Since

1

the same issues repeated themselves, I wrote notes to save me rewriting the information every time I needed to explain something. Those notes, written to address the common issues I found in authors' works, became more comprehensive over time, and now form the basis of this book.

I will only touch lightly on the big picture aspects of fiction writing, and apart from clarifying a few confusions that I see often, I won't be dealing with grammar and punctuation—plenty of books cover those topics. This book focuses primarily on line editing skills.

I am grateful to the many teachers I've had and would, in particular, like to thank Australian editor Selena Hanet-Hutchins for her tuition, and author Laurie Stiller for his tips. Thank you also to the many online sources written by a variety of tutors more knowledgeable than I, in particular, Kristen Lamb, Roz Morris, Jacqui Murray and Jami Gold for their informative blogs on a variety of writing topics. To Mary Maddox, Brent Meske and Angela M. Blount who read this book before publication and gave valuable suggestions, thank you. And a special thanks to Angela for her concise summary of the elements of a professional book review.

Also a thank you to Kevin Berry for his excellent editing job and his encouragement to extend the book beyond my initial ideas.

I would also like to thank the Awesome Indies reviewers—too numerous to mention individually, but you know who you are—for their support in my writing journey and in particular for helping me to help authors improve their writing.

I hope you find this book helpful, for that is my intention in writing it.

1

Introduction

Before we get down to details, I'd like to set the background against which I wrote this book. Some authors can get quite emotional about anything that looks remotely like a rule, and I'd like to reassure these authors that dictating a set way of writing is not my aim here. These points are purely for authors' education, something for them to understand so that they can apply these tips where and when appropriate.

What Makes Good Prose?

"Beautiful writing is when every word is the right word, in its right place and there for a reason. There is nothing extraneous. The words flow so smoothly that the reader is transported beyond the words. They even forget they are reading." Elizabeth Weiss, publisher at Allen and Unwin, Australia.

"Good writing is supposed to evoke sensation in the reader

— not the fact that it is raining, but the feeling of being rained upon." E.L. Doctorow, author of *Billy Bathgate.*

"Writers we in time call 'great' tend to follow all the rules of good writing. Spare, interesting, easy to read, easy to understand to the point we forget that we are reading." G J Berger, award-winning author of *South of Burnt Rocks, West of the Moon.*

Everyone has a different answer to the question of what makes good writing, but all point to the same elements: a smooth read with nothing that pulls you out of the story or makes you aware that you're reading, well-chosen words and no extraneous ones, and a variety of sentence structures with a clear meaning and interesting rhythm.

What isn't good writing is anything that makes you go 'eh?' or 'huh?' or that seems clumsy. Anything that makes you aware of the words is not good writing, and that includes anything that comes across as pretentious. That's why writing coaches advise not to try to impress and not to use big words when simple ones will do.

The next question is: How do you write good prose? But answering this question raises a few issues, because as soon as you start to lay out guidelines, people will turn them into rules and stick by them even when they aren't appropriate, so we need to address this first.

Rules or Guidelines?

The human mind has a tendency to see things dualistically. We assume that if this thing is good, then its opposite must be bad, and if this thing is bad, it must always be bad. We also have a tendency to solidify ideas so that a general suggestion, in our mind, becomes a hard and fast rule. If we are to avoid these traps, we need to examine our assumptions.

Writing is an area where we can see this at work. Don't consider these principles as prescriptive rules to be followed slavishly. They are guidelines to help us make our prose better, and they can be ignored when character voice dictates that it would sound wrong.

If you think of these tips as rules, you may find them restrictive. You may feel that if you pay them too much attention your creativity will be compromised, but the restriction is in your mind, not in the guidelines themselves. The idea is to use these guidelines in a way that will help, not hinder you. Don't concern yourself with them on your first draft when you're just trying to get the story out while the inspiration is flowing. Use them at the self-editing stage to turn your telling into showing, to tighten up your prose and make it more interesting, and use them as a diagnostic tool to help you work out why a scene isn't as powerful as it should be.

What I'm sharing here are guidelines, not rules; though how you apply them is important. However, there are rules for grammar and punctuation, and if you break them, you run the risk of being misunderstood. You'll also look like an amateur and have your book rejected in disgust by anyone who recognises your mistakes.

At the same time, some aspects of punctuation are flexible, and it is important to know where those areas are. You must know the difference between 'its' and 'it's', 'their' and 'there', 'reign' and 'rein' and so on, but in some respects, UK English usage differs from US English usage, and publishers' style guides vary in some areas. For example, UK/Australian English style guides allow fewer commas than the more prescriptive *Chicago Manual of Style*, and leave out many of the periods that Americans use in abbreviations—I'm using Australian conventions here. The important thing is to be consistent with your usage throughout, and the overriding factor in 'correctness' is whether the usage makes the meaning clear or obscures it, and whether it adds or detracts from the flow and rhythm of the reading experience.

Em dashes and semicolons have clear rules that you should not ignore, but they do have various uses, and where one editor may use an em dash, another may use a semicolon and neither may be wrong. Also, grammar usage does change with the times; for example, split infinitives are acceptable these days where the unsplit version sounds weird, but the correct form should still be used where it sounds okay—why not? Fragments are seen as a valid way to add rhythmical emphasis to prose and maintain naturalness in dialogue. In dialogue the authenticity of the characters' speech patterns always has precedence over grammar rules. Modern people speak in contractions, so use them.

If you're already a well-known author, you might be able to get away with flaunting writing rules; for example, Tim Winton, a popular Australian author, didn't use any speech marks in his book *Breath*. I found it made the book difficult to read, and it made me very aware of the writing, but his publisher accepted it and, therefore, so did the reading public. But he isn't a self-published author fighting the stigma of poor writing. Even if you can get away with it, why ignore convention unless you have a very good reason? Perhaps I missed something, but the lack of quotation marks in Mr Winton's book detracted from the story, at least for me, and the only reason one should flaunt convention is if it improves the book. Perhaps he simply wanted to make a statement. Clearly, he has the status to do so, but most of us don't.

Guidelines, such as those in this book, steer us away from overusing certain things and help us to see options that may be more interesting and more evocative than what we might write in our first draft. I don't see the points I outline here as rules, more as warnings. I'm not saying that you should never use the constructions I suggest you avoid; I'm saying your writing will be better if you don't use them too often. Frankly, though, ignoring this kind of advice risks quick rejection from publishers, possibly even before they finish the first chapter.

There are fashions in style too. Active rather than passive writing is a modern style—more about that later. You can ignore modern trends, but unless you write your old style extremely well, be prepared to not rate so well against books that do follow the trends, because trends are a response to reader preferences. After studying this book, you should understand how to make your action sequences come alive. Ignore active writing in such scenes and your writing is likely to appear lacklustre.

There are tips to help us lay out our novels. For example, those that help us see if our first page has the elements needed to hook the readers. I wouldn't set out to write a first page according to the tips, I'd write the story and then check that it did grab the readers; if it didn't, then I'd look at the tips.

Tips for structuring plots, developing characters, writing realistic dialogue and so on abound in writing books and on the internet, and tips on writing good prose follows. I see all of these as tools, not rules, to be used where they are relevant and discarded where they aren't. The skill of the author and editor is in knowing where they are relevant. The understanding comes from reading widely and recognising what works and what doesn't. My advice is to use these tips when self-editing your work and discover what they do to your writing; after a while, you will naturally use them where necessary and ignore them when there is a reason for an alternative.

Perhaps some people naturally write excellent prose from the beginning. I wasn't one of those people, but through applying the principles in this book, my writing improved enormously. After self-editing five novels and editing numerous novels for others, I no longer need to consciously apply these elements when I write. Their use is natural to me now, as is the intuitive understanding of where they do not apply. It's the same as dancing; everyone can dance, but studying and practising the technique of dancing transforms your dancing from that of an amateur to that of a professional. Once internalised, the technique enhances the dancer's creativity.

Follow Your Gut, But ...

If these are not rules, how do you know when to apply them and when not to?

Follow your gut feeling ... but ... make sure you're listening to the right feeling.

The gut feeling you need to follow is the part of you that knows. Often it's the part we don't want to hear, so we don't really listen. We pretend to listen, but what we hear is laziness or defensiveness in disguise. Perhaps we don't want to do the work required to go through our manuscript one more time, or we're impatient to say it's finished, or we don't want to do what someone else tells us to do, so we ignore the shimmer of unease in the pit of our stomach. We push it away and pretend it isn't there, but that's the feeling we need to listen to, the one that tells us whether what we've written sounds right or not.

Passive Writing is Not the Same as Passive Voice

Though I do sometimes appear to use them as such, the terms passive writing and passive prose are not synonymous with 'telling'. However, they do contribute to it, so in some cases, what applies to one also applies to the other. Active prose is less likely to have a 'told' feel even when you are telling. The important distinction to make is that the terms passive writing and passive prose do not refer to passive voice. Passive voice is only one example of passive prose.

According to Wikipedia, passive **voice** is where:

'The grammatical subject expresses the theme or patient of the main verb—that is, the person or thing that undergoes the action or has its state changed. This contrasts with active voice, in which the subject has the agent role.

'For example, in the passive sentence *"The tree was pulled down"*, the subject (*the tree*) denotes the patient rather than the agent of the action. In contrast, the sentences *"Someone pulled down the tree"* and *"The tree is down"* are active sentences.' http://en.wikipedia.org/wiki/Passive_voice

Another way of identifying passive voice is where the subject that does the action *is not specified or is placed before the action.* Note the passive voice in italics in the previous sentence. It's stronger to have a specific subject up front. *E.g. Prose is particularly passive where the author does not specify the subject that does the action, or they place it after the action.* Passive voice is not grammatically incorrect and is useful where you wish to remove ownership of an action, or make something sound remote and authoritative, but when used generally in fiction, it is simply not very exciting, and prose peppered with it soon becomes dull.

But passive writing is more than just the use of passive voice. Your writing can be free of passive voice as defined above and still be passive writing. The trouble with passive writing is that it isn't as engaging as active writing. It isn't immediate, meaning that it doesn't seem to be happening now, and it doesn't draw the reader into the action. The scene itself may be dramatic, but the writing leaves the reader outside the characters and the events. Such writing is uninviting, or rather cold, like a blind date with nothing to say. If you're ever reading something that, despite feeling as if it should, just isn't holding you, it may be because the writing is passive.

Passive writing is common from beginning writers and in self-published books that haven't had a line editor. It was how I wrote before I knew better, and my early drafts of the *Diamond Peak* series were full of it. I don't write like that anymore, and I'm very glad that I learned not to before I published my books. The rest of this section will give you the information you need to write active prose—albeit expressed only briefly.

Good Writing is More Than Good Grammar

Good grammar does not always equal good writing.

What? With all the fuss that people make over editing these days, it's easy to lose sight of the writing because we're too busy looking at the grammar and punctuation. The old saying that expresses this is: you can't see the forest for the trees.

This is why a copy edit is not enough to ensure that writing is of a professional standard. A copy edit focuses only on the trees. It will check that each tree is straight and well pruned, but there is more to a beautiful forest than straight trees. The occasional bent, cracked or fallen one adds interest and variety, but if most of them are broken, the forest is a mess we can't negotiate, or it is so ugly that we don't want to go there. Vines, ferns, epiphytes and shrubs add colour and texture, but too many of them obscure the trees, make the forest impenetrable and, at the very least, throw us into sensory overload. Clumped together, they prevent us from seeing any one of them to its best advantage.

In this analogy, the straight trees are grammatically correct sentences. The bent, broken and twisted ones are the more fluid parts of our language, things that have changed, or are in the process of changing or, though strictly speaking grammatically incorrect, can be used stylistically to good effect or to reflect modern speech and cultural differences.

The split infinitive is one example. Since we mostly speak in split infinitives now, to insist on writing without the splits is petty and will sound wrong in situations where informal speech is required. The fragment is another example; although traditionally grammatically incorrect, we often speak in fragments, and their judicious use in written English, even outside of speech, adds punch and rhythm to writing. Writing dialogue in dialect also breaks grammatical and spelling conventions (note that I don't call them rules) but it adds colour and reality. Overused, however, it becomes difficult to read.

It's usually pretty clear to any experienced reviewer where ignoring grammatical convention works and where it doesn't. Where it works, it improves the reading experience. Where it doesn't, it diminishes it. Where used in ignorance, it appears clumsy; where used knowingly, it adds texture and style. It is safer for the beginning writer to stick to the conventions, but not so fanatically that they apply conventions indiscriminately and remove all personality from their writing: for example, continually using 'is not' where 'isn't' would be more appropriate for the tone and style of the work.

The under story of shrubs, ferns, epiphytes and vines are an analogy for adverbs, adjectives, metaphors, similes, euphemisms, alliteration, allusion, personification, paradox, understatement and other stylistic devices. Well placed and used judiciously, these add to the reading experience, but overused or badly placed, no matter how grammatically correct, they detract.

A whole forest of straight trees planted in straight lines without vines, under story or ferns and so on, could be an analogy for a technical writing style incorrectly applied to fiction, or for grammatically correct sentences that do not vary in their construction and are so void of embellishments that the reading experience is quite dull. It could also refer to an awesome science fiction novel where the bare language expresses the aliens' personalities perfectly. It's not a matter of right or wrong, but of how you use the tools available and for what effect.

Passive writing can be grammatically correct, which is why a copy editor will not 'fix' it, but too much of it makes the prose flat and unengaging. Sentences beginning with participial phrases (starting with words ending in 'ing') are grammatically correct—so long as the participial phrase is attached to an agent—but when overused, it is the mark of a hack writer. And it's the same for beginning sentences with prepositional phrases prefixed with the word 'as'.

It is the line editor's job to do this kind of landscaping, and a good one is aware of the current trends in writing. Of course, you can ignore current trends, such as the preference for active over passive constructions, but you need to be aware of the point of the convention that you're ignoring. In this case it's that active writing is generally more immediate and engaging than the passive form.

The writer's challenge is to use good grammar well, while feeling free to occasionally and judiciously use what strict traditionalists might consider incorrect grammar. We need to remember that grammatical conventions change as our language changes, and that what is acceptable varies according to local usage, and not be too picky over what may be outdated conventions, but at the same time we should not disregard grammatical conventions for no good reason.

As with most things in life, it's a matter of balance.

Attitude is Important

When we start out as artists of any kind, we tend to be protective of our work and highly sensitive to criticism. Though this attitude is natural in the early stages of a career in the creative arts, it is not a helpful one. It makes it harder for you to see problems with your work. Also, if your friends feel they have to pussyfoot around your ego, it will be hard for them to give you the kind of feedback you need, and you won't hear it even if they do give it.

A defensive attitude is born of insecurity that comes from lack of knowledge and lack of self-esteem, so the more you write and self-evaluate, the more feedback and knowledge you acquire; and the more confident you become with your own skills, the more this attitude will soften. But we can speed that process up by cultivating a more mature and helpful attitude from the beginning.

We have to believe that all criticism will make our work better, and we need to understand that the point of editorial suggestion is not to criticise the work, but to improve it. Of course, we must criticise it in order to improve it, but don't get hung up on the criticism; remember its purpose:

Criticism helps us improve the work. If no one tells us what doesn't work, we won't make it better. And we do want to write well, don't we? Besides, it comes with the territory; if you publish a book, expect criticism. There's a whole chapter on handling criticism near the end of this book.

Objectivity and detachment are the mark of a good self-editor. You need to separate yourself from your work. Your book is not you; it's just something you're working on. Reading and reviewing a lot of other people's books—choose well-written ones—are good for learning to see your own work objectively.

The aim of this book is to help you write better prose. I can give you the information, but you must develop the attitude that will allow you to benefit from it.

Voice

Your voice as an author is your perspective on the world as it expresses itself through your writing. It's the kind of things you write about, the way you write about them, and the kind of language structures and words you use because they feel right to you. Your voice is what makes your writing unique, and it often takes many books before your voice settles into something consistent.

Some authors think that paying attention to the kinds of guidelines for active/good prose that I present here will water down their voice, but in fact the opposite is true; their use strengthens your prose and so strengthens your voice. If your writing is expressed better, your voice will be expressed better also. These points do not change your words, they change how well you present them and how well readers respond to them.

Our characters, when written in an intimate point of view, also have a voice. A strong character voice is engaging in itself, and if strong enough can make some guidelines irrelevant or, at least, less relevant. (Perhaps this is why Tim Winton was able to do away with quotation marks.) However, you should never use this, or the 'but-this-is-my-style' argument as a defence mechanism against informed criticism. As artists, we must put aside our ego if we are ever to achieve our full potential.

A writer's voice is what makes everything they write sound like their writing. It's when your writing, no matter what the topic, expresses your view of the world in an identifiable style. Something written in your voice will sound 'right' to you when you read it aloud, so test it that way and follow your instincts. A strong voice, if it's a highly captivating one, can carry a work that ignores fashions and stylistic recommendations.

At the same time, remember that the human mind has a tendency to see things dualistically, so don't use the importance of establishing your voice as an excuse to ignore the advice of countless writing coaches. Used properly, they will enhance your voice, not diminish it.

In the words of some of my editing clients:

"Tahlia helped me see a pattern of passive writing in my books that I'd originally considered simply my writer's voice. With each submission, my writing style improved and my prose became more confident and powerful. My voice is stronger than it's ever been." Welcome Cole.

"Tahlia somehow managed to keep the idea of every sentence, keep my voice but make it much better." Dorian Zari.

Editing Necessity and Process

Anyone can write a book and, these days, anyone can publish one, but not everyone can do it well. My experience as an Awesome Indies reviewer has shown me just how difficult it is to produce a quality self-published book without professional help, but not everyone can afford the help they need.

Writing a book is very time consuming; editing a book is the same, and anyone editing your work must be paid for their time, so professional editing, even at the cheapest rates, costs a significant amount of money—though some editors will do a 50/50 deal, a kind of learn as you go process. The unfortunate truth is that it can take a long time to make that money back, and there is no guarantee that you will ever get it back. That's why self-publishers are reticent to engage professionals. But can you afford not to?

Though it's true that many readers don't notice sloppy writing and poor editing, most book bloggers and certainly the major review sites do, and in this highly competitive market, only the best authors will survive in the long term. Readers are becoming more discerning, and eventually sloppy writers will fall by the wayside. If you're planning on making a career out of writing, you need to make sure that you're writing well. Besides:

If it's worth doing, it's worth doing well.

Isn't it?

If you think that your story is strong enough to publish, then the least you can invest in it is the desire to do it well. Motivation inspires the actions required to achieve a desired outcome. So:

Motivation is important. Aim to write well.

Most new authors—like me when I started—find themselves inspired with an idea and start writing without any training. They only learn to write through writing, and doing workshops and courses, and reading books and reputable blogs on writing. That's fine; first drafts should never concern themselves with technique. First drafts are all about getting that inspiration down in black and white. But to create a quality product, subsequent drafts require the application of knowledge and skill in the craft of writing.

If you don't have the skills yourself, you employ someone who does, and even if you do have the skills yourself, you still have to employ someone to check your work.

We cannot fully edit our own work.

We simply don't see it the way others do. We know what we're trying to say, but our readers don't, so someone with no prior knowledge of the story must do the final edit.

But we can self-edit as part of the writing process.

The more editing we do ourselves, the less someone else has to do, and the less it will cost us, but we need to learn the necessary skills.

The best way to learn is to pay a professional to do a comprehensive edit on your book—don't worry about the cost, consider it education. You're unlikely to make the money back in the short term, but it's an investment in your career that you can't afford not to make. Better than one editor is to engage a team of two or three editors to work on your book so you get more than one opinion—it shouldn't cost more. When you go through the edits, look closely at them, and learn from them. If you don't know why something has been done and the editor hasn't told you, ask why the changes have been made. (See appendix one for how to find the right editor for you.)

If you can't afford to hire your own tutor in the form of an editor, you're back to courses and reading for your tuition. The best book I've ever come across on the topic of self-editing is *Self-Editing for Fiction Writers,*

Second Edition: How to Edit Yourself Into Print. by Renni Brown and Dave King.

However you do it, your book needs to go through the following editing process.

Structural/conceptual/developmental edit: This is the big stuff—plot, character, structure, concept, world building and so on. A manuscript appraisal or beta readers who are writers or editors can fulfil this stage of the process. There are plenty of books on writing that cover this area.

Line edit: This stage cuts the clutter and improves the prose. It's the least understood area of writing and the form of editing most lacking in indie books. It is also the focus of this book, and once an author has the skills they can do most of this themselves. If you learn the elements of good prose, your line editing costs will be minimal.

Copy edit: corrects grammar, punctuation and spelling, and checks for consistency.

Proof-read: checks the above and picks up typos.

If you want your book to look professional and meet the standards of mainstream books, then don't miss the line edit.

2

The Broad Sweep

In this section, I take a brief look at the 'big picture' aspects of fiction writing. Here I focus on the aspects that I often find lacking, or not well understood, in books presented to me for appraisal or review. Check these points first when evaluating your book at the self-editing stage.

Plot

It's amazing how many books I see that don't have the basics of plot. We can be so familiar with our story that we don't see the gigantic hole staring us in the face. A novel without a plot is not a novel at all, so we must check that before anything. When you first sit back and look at your story, ask yourself the following:

Who is my protagonist (main character)? If there is more than one main character, you still need to have one major one that the reader can follow and really get to know.

Are they introduced first? Introduce them straight up, so the reader knows immediately *who* the story is about.

What is my protagonist's aim in this story? What is their task, the central problem they must solve? What must they achieve, solve, fix, or discover? If your protagonist has no clear aim or challenge, you don't have a story. Their aim tells the reader *what* the story is about, and it should be clear to the reader by somewhere around the 15% mark. Leave it later than 25% of the way in and you'll likely have lost readers. They might know who the story is about, but they won't know what it's about until you reveal the protagonist's task.

Who or what is preventing them from achieving their aim? This is the all important antagonist. Without this, you also have no story, because you have no tension. A story about someone searching for a package is not enough—there has to be someone or something trying to prevent them from finding that package. The antagonist can be non-human, like a fear or physical terrain, but your work will be stronger if you have a person involved because people are unpredictable.

If you have these in place, you have the basics. After that, look at the story arc. Does the tension rise, the challenges increase until the point of resolution? Does each chapter have its own tension?

Check also that each scene is actually necessary in the book. Every scene should move the story forward and should have at least two (some say three) reasons for being there. Be ruthless; if it doesn't move the story forward, cut it. You can always incorporate parts of it into other scenes.

The best information on plot that I've found is from Micheal Hauge, who talks about the elements of plot as they're used in successful screen plays. These apply equally to fiction, and his 6 Stage Plot Structure provides a good way to check that your story does have the elements that will keep a reader reading.

If you're writing literary fiction, you may scoff at the idea of using a screenplay checklist, thinking that it isn't relevant to your work, but if your plot is strong, experience has shown me that it will naturally fall into his stages whether you meant it to or not, so it's a good idea to look at your plot in light of it; it may give you ideas that will take your book to another level.

Point of View

Check that the point of view (POV) you write from is consistent and that any changes between points of view don't cause confusion. Point of view refers to the viewpoint taken by the narrator of the story. We write through their eyes.

First person—written from the perspective of one person. This POV uses the pronouns 'me', 'myself' and 'I', e.g. *I ran down the street. He chased me.* This person cannot know other people's thoughts, emotions and motivations except as they see them reflected in the other people's expressions and actions. They can assume, but they can't think someone else's thoughts. Neither can they know what is hiding around the corner or what is in a place they haven't been to before. It's perfectly acceptable to write different chapters in different characters' voices in first person, but put the character's name in the chapter title and make sure you make it clear in the first sentence whose POV you're in. I wouldn't try for more than two in this fashion though, and it's more appropriate for young adult and romances than other genres.

Second person —addresses the reader. This POV uses the pronouns 'you', 'your' and 'yours'. We use these three pronouns when addressing one, or more than one, person. Second person is used for e-mail messages,

31

presentations, and business and technical writing. You may also see it used in blog posts.

Third person—written from the perspective of a third person. This POV uses the pronouns 'he', 'she' and 'they'; eg, *He ran down the street.* There are two kinds of third person points of view:

Omniscient—written from the perspective of an all-knowing narrator. They know what everyone is thinking and feeling and what is hiding around the corner. Omniscient POV is not often used these days because it keeps the reader one step removed from the feelings of the characters. It is most often seen in epic fantasy. The important thing to understand when writing in omniscient POV is there should be only one voice, that of the narrator, and even though they can see the thoughts of every character, it is advisable not to try to explain many different characters' thought processes in one scene because it quickly becomes confusing for the reader. I suggest that beginning writers avoid this point of view. It's too remote for many modern readers, less immediate than the alternatives and hard to do well.

Third person close/intimate/limited—written from the perspective of a character and in that character's voice but using the pronoun 'he' or 'she' to refer to him or her. The language used is what that character would use if they were telling the story, so the reader sees the action through the character's eyes. This is used when an author wants to be able to show more than one perspective on the story, but wants the reader to identify more deeply with a character than is possible in omniscient. For this reason, it usually involves changing from one intimate point of view to another, and this is where the writing can fall into head-hopping.

Which approach you take is entirely up to you. The important thing is to make any POV changes clear to the reader.

Head-hopping

Many readers don't notice head-hopping unless it's really chronic, but writing is better without it, and it's a common trap for new writers. Some writers maintain that whether or not you head-hop is a personal preference rather than an indication of quality, but head-hopping definitely does weaken the writing.

People aren't always clear about what head-hopping means, so it's important that we clarify that. Let us start with what head-hopping isn't.

The term head-hopping does NOT refer to point of view changes that occur:

• Chapter by chapter, i.e. one chapter in one POV

and another chapter in a different POV;

- Scene by scene changes in POV where it is obvious that the scene has changed;

- As one clearly delineated additional POV within a scene, i.e. a switch from the POV of the main character to a secondary character—and back again if necessary. This is common in romance novels where it is important for the reader to understand the different perspectives of the man and the woman. Clearly delineated means that the change is obvious, and there is no confusion. Sometimes it's marked by a blank line or it's simply written like a smooth baton change. However, if the switch is only for one sentence, or involves several different characters, then no matter how well it's done, the writing would be better off without it;

- A narrator telling the reader what a character is thinking in omniscient point of view is not head-hopping so long as the writing remains in the omniscient narrator's voice and it is clear whose perspective the narrator is relating. In true omniscient POV there is only one voice, that of the narrator. Although this all-knowing voice of the narrator knows what everyone is thinking, s/he tells the story from a perspective that is external to them and in his/her voice, not in the character's voice or from their perspective.

The term head-hopping specifically refers to:

- Non-delineated changes of POV within a scene that move quickly between characters (i.e. one sentence or a short paragraph, then back again, or to another character), especially if it's between more than two characters, happens often, or uses the POV of minor characters who have limited POV throughout the rest of the story. Valid changes of POV are limited to main characters and are clearly delineated.

How to Achieve a Smooth Baton Change Between POVs

The first POV character turns their attention to the second character in some way, either through thoughts, gaze or action. Alternatively, the first POV character could leave the scene.

The first sentence of the new POV also mentions the new POV character's name and their thoughts or feelings about something. They should be distinctly related to the new character so there is no possible chance that these thoughts could be attributed to the previous character.

A paragraph or more of omniscient POV is also a way to create a break between different third person close POVs.

What's Wrong With Head-hopping?

Head-hopping weakens the writing. It can result in readers having to reread passages to work out whose point of view they are currently following. This drags them out of the story, and they lose engagement.

Reading many people's viewpoints of one scene can make the writing less immediate and engaging by:

- Slowing down the action;

- Taking the reader away from the main point, thus watering down the impact of the scene;

- Creating a barrier between the reader and the story. It's as if you're always dodging around the action instead of meeting it head on;

- Using the thoughts of a variety of characters as a way to tell the reader things instead of showing them through the eyes of the main character. It's another form of 'lazy' writing;

- Giving the reader a general sense of confusion or lack of clarity about the scene;

- Giving the reader more info than they need. This bloats the scene and leaves little to the reader's imagination, which dulls the writing.

Usually the scene and all the characters' feelings can be effectively described or at least sufficiently hinted at through the point of view of the person the reader followed into the scene. If a change of POV is needed to give insight into a secondary character, then it should be only one other character in any one scene and there should be a clear delineation between the views. Either with or without the blank line, the first sentence must make it very clear that the point of view has changed. Even when the change flows smoothly, it is preferable that it happens only once in a scene (i.e. change to secondary character and back again). Basically, the more you change POV, the greater the chance for confusion.

Examples

An example of head-hopping:

'It's raining outside,' George said. So much for getting the washing dry today.

'It's not too heavy, though.' Sally stared into the dusk. Would George stay and get pizza with her? She turned and fixed her eyes on his, hoping.

'I need to go. I have washing on the line.' George stood,

37

uncomfortable under her intense gaze. Didn't she realise how needy she appeared?

'It's too late now. It'll be soaked.' Please don't go; don't go. I need you. She reached for his hand. 'Let's have pizza.'

He shook his head, suddenly desperate to leave.

One way to write the same scene without the head-hopping.

This is now all described from George's point of view. The same points come across without the head-hopping, so nothing is gained by the head-hopping.

'It's raining outside,' George said. So much for getting the washing dry today.

'It's not too heavy, though.' Sally stared into the dusk, then turned and fixed her eyes on his.

'I need to go. I have washing on the line.' George stood, uncomfortable under her intense gaze. Didn't she realise how needy she appeared?

'It's too late now. It'll be soaked.' She reached for his hand. 'Please, stay. We can have pizza.'

He shook his head, suddenly desperate to leave.

An example of a successful change of point of view.

This excerpt from my book *Lethal Inheritance* introduces the secondary character—the love interest—for the first time. My first attempts at writing this—it was my first book—had me head-hopping all over the place giving the reader whiplash as I tried to show both characters' feelings and reactions to their initial contact. I solved the problem by having the first paragraph in Nick's point of view talk about the reaction he'd just had.

Just before the change, Ariel turns the reader's attention onto Nick by wondering what he felt. The change is made by beginning the next sentence with Nick's name and him answering the question Ariel asked herself. The gap between, though not strictly necessary, gives the reader a clear indication that some change has occurred.

The man, tall and—Ariel noted appreciatively—athletically built, pushed off the tree with a smile that softened the sharp angles of his square jaw and straight nose. He looked older than her by several years—twentyish, she decided.

'Hi, I'm Nick,' he said in a pleasant voice.

Ariel met his gaze and a blast of energy shot from his eyes into hers. It raced into the centre of her chest and exploded, knocking her breathless. She wrenched her eyes from his and staggered backwards.

'What the hell?' She felt as if he'd bludgeoned her with a blunt instrument. 'What was that?'

'What was what?' He sounded completely innocent, and his expression, though a little tense, was carefully neutral, but he wouldn't meet her eyes.

Had he really not felt anything?

Nick wondered how she'd managed to wrench open a door in his chest and unleash a burst of that unspeakable power. It'd raced up his spine and out his eyes, and after he'd torn his gaze from hers, it'd taken all his concentration to shut the door and keep the rest safely locked up. The girl was dangerous.

'Nothing,' she muttered and hurried past him, breaking his self-absorption and reminding him that he had a job to do.

'Wait, I'm going that way too.' He raced after her. 'Can I walk with you?'

'No.' She sounded pissed off.

Part of him wanted to ask if he'd hurt her, but the wise part told him to shut the hell up. He didn't want to have to deal with it now. Actually, not ever. 'I'm not going to hurt you.'

'Really? So far you don't inspire me with confidence.'

'I'm sorry, okay.' He wanted to say it wouldn't happen again, but he couldn't guarantee it.

She stopped and looked at him. 'So you did do something.'

He avoided her gaze. 'I didn't do anything.'

'Fine. Whatever.' She walked on. 'Just leave me alone, all right.'

Well, that worked out well, he thought sarcastically, and followed her in uneasy silence.

Tense

The tense of a verb tells us when an action has taken place. I'm not going to go into the grammatical side of tenses—your copy editor will pick up any inconsistencies—the important thing in terms of the big picture that we're looking at here is choosing the tense in which to write your book.

Novels can be written in:

- Present tense: He jumps. (Action happens as the sentence is spoken.)

- Past tense: He jumped. (Action happened before the sentence was spoken.)

The other basic tense is simple future tense: He will jump. (Action expected to occur after the sentence is spoken). This tense is used as part of normal story-telling in books written in either of the above tenses. A character or narrator can talk about what he or she expects to happen in the future, just as they can use past tense when talking about the past. But in terms of the overall tense of the story, the general advice is to stick to whatever you've chosen. So don't use present tense in one sentence or paragraph and past tense in the next.

But story-telling is changing, and in stories with different story threads and viewpoints there may be reasons for having a different tense for a different chapter or character. If you choose to do this, you need to be very clear about why you've done it and what the effect is. It's too easy to make a confusing mess.

Present tense has become more popular in the last few years. I expect it's because of the immediacy it gives to the story, but be careful. It's not easy to do a good job of using present tense, and some readers find it very annoying or get tired of it easily. So ask yourself why you've chosen this tense, and whether it is a good reason.

Present tense also lends itself to having some sections in past tense. This is still a little radical, but a break from present tense can be refreshing, and it can underscore time differences and make distinctions. For instance, if you choose to insert reports or letters and so on into your story, they won't be in present tense.

I chose present tense for the base story in my *Prunella Smith series,* but one of the stories within the primary story is told in past tense. This is because it's a novel that Prunella (Ella) is editing. I needed to differentiate the novel she was working on from what was happening in Ella's life, so I chose two different tenses. Each story thread, however, sticks to its own tense.

I also used past tense when Ella wanted to distance herself from an event, so a dream could be written in present tense if I wanted the reader to experience it as she experienced it, but if she remembered it after she woke up, I'd write it in past tense.

Another valid use of changing tenses in a story written primarily in present tense is if you have a story thread that takes place in the past. The part of the story set now can be in present tense and the part that took place in 1976 could be in past tense.

But be careful, apart from there needing to be a valid reason for different tense usage, each change should be in a separate section and that section and story thread should stick to the same tense throughout. It's a bit like head-hopping in that too many changes in quick succession give a reader whiplash.

I said earlier that writing in present tense is not easy, and I advise new writers not to attempt it. Why? Basically because it's all too easy to overuse variations of the verb 'to be' (the reasons for why that's not a good thing come later in this book) and because it can easily come out choppy and sounding like something a child might write. If you want choppy and childish, that's fine, but you can do both in past tense in a more sophisticated way and without having to be stuck in it for the whole book.

Present tense works okay in first person because you're asking the reader to experience the central character's story as it happens; you want the reader to be very aware that it is happening now, in this timeframe, and you want them to be right in the story and fully identified with the character. Those seem like valid reasons for choosing this tense. Novels can be written in third person present, of course, but I think third person generally works better in past tense.

So if you're an inexperienced author and you've chosen present tense, it might be a good exercise to try rewriting a passage in past tense. If the prose flows better, consider writing the whole book in past tense. Don't use present tense just because you think it's fashionable!

Tension

Tension is what keeps a reader reading. Without tension a novel will be somewhat dull and easy to put down. Some say that there should be tension on every page; I'm not sure that's completely necessary unless you're writing a thriller, but the statement does make you realise just how important tension is. There should be tension in every chapter, though. And the book as a whole should have tension as the driving force.

A strong plot with clear goals and an antagonist will provide the overall tension to hold a work of fiction together and keep the reader turning pages, and though every chapter can also have the same kind of aim, thwarting of aim and question as to whether the protagonist will be successful in achieving their aim or not, there are other ways to create tension. I became familiar with these during my time in theatre and particularly when I taught drama, because we're talking about dramatic tension here.

Dramatic tension is created through the following:

- Conflict (as in basic plot structure)—the question is: who will win?

- Tension of the task—the protagonist has a task to complete and the question is: will they complete the task?

- Tension of relationships—this is the kind of tension we have in romances. Relationships have problems and challenges. The question is: will they solve their problems and get back together?

- Mystery—something is unexplained, and it's important to the protagonist that they solve the mystery. The question is: who did it? Or, what is s/he hiding? And other such questions.

- Humour—humour keeps us reading, particularly when it occurs through the unexpected.

- Surprise—surprises and plot twists keep the reader intrigued. The question here is: what will happen next? Surprises at the end of chapters work well, and a surprise at the end of a short story can transform an otherwise ordinary story.

If your chapters have one or more of these kinds of dramatic tension, your readers will keep reading. Though a particular kind of book may focus on one of these, a good book will use several of them, perhaps all of them. Every one you use will increase the tension in the pages and will make your book harder to put down.

A book doesn't need to have a fast pace to be something one can't put down, it simply needs to have tension. So when you look over what you've written, ask yourself:

what creates tension in this chapter or scene? If you don't find anything, ask yourself why that section is there. The reason should give you an angle on what kind of tension should be in the chapter or scene. If you find no reason for it, then it's not needed and you should delete it. The other way to work here is to simply ask yourself how you could angle the chapter to create some more tension.

The general rule for adding tension is to make things more difficult for your characters. Be mean to them. Add stumbling blocks. Don't make everything too easy. Life isn't like that, and good fiction reflects life.

Transitions

Stories are made up from a series of scenes, and how we move the reader from one scene to another is important. In general, we want the story to flow smoothly and the reader to be clear on who they're following, and where they are in time and place.

Even if you aim for a disjointed feel, you don't want to confuse your reader. You have to give them something to hang onto, some way to piece the scenes together. Otherwise the book will come across as a mess. Our brains look for meaning. When they don't find it, things don't make sense, and readers generally like their books to make sense.

In books that shift across time, space and characters, it's a good idea to head a chapter or section with the date, place and character the scene is about, e.g. James. Sydney. September 1951.

Often connecting scenes simply requires a sentence that starts with something like: 'Two days later …' or 'They drove to the beach and …' or 'When he arrived at school …' These kinds of connecting sentences or paragraphs are one place where 'telling' is better than 'showing'. We actually don't need to know every step the characters took to get them to the next important event, so a summary is all we need.

If you don't like this style of transition or don't consider it necessary to mention the events or time frame between the main scenes—perhaps you're aiming for a choppy, cinematic style in the book—you still need to give the reader sufficient information to enable them to make the connections themselves.

Movies jump from scene to scene and the viewer follows without the need for transitions because we instantly get the information we need from the visuals. If you're taking the same approach in your fiction, then you need to provide the same kind of cues immediately at the start of the scene.

So if you're going for that style, then make sure that your scene changes start with the POV character's name in the first sentence (if it's different to the POV character in the previous scene), along with something in the first paragraph that sets the scene in time and place. I explain more about this in the section on writing like a movie.

Showing and Telling

When you look over your work after your first draft, note the scenes and sections that are 'told' rather than 'shown'. Mark them, decide which parts need to be shown rather than told, then go back and re-write those sections. For maximum impact, you'll want to make sure your action scenes are shown and, for the modern reader, it's advisable to have considerably more showing than telling in the book overall.

What Telling Is

Telling has a narrator between the reader and the action, so the reader stands outside the action and somewhat remote from the character. Readers are constantly reminded that they are reading, because the narrator tells us that the character did, saw, heard or felt something. Telling also talks about something that happened in the past, so the scene has little immediacy. Telling can cover a lot of ground quickly, so it's useful for non-pivotal connecting scenes.

Telling is a natural part of omniscient point of view because it's written from the POV of a narrator rather than the POV of a character, so the reader is always one step removed from the action. This means that authors writing in this POV need to write well if they are to fully engage their readers. They also need to understand what they're giving up in terms of immediacy when they choose omniscient POV. Telling can be considered a stylistic choice for those who know what they're doing, but unless the telling is done well, books that are all telling are generally not as engaging as those that have a balance between showing and telling.

Poorly written expositional prose (telling) is usually passive, but there's nothing passive about the following excerpt, an example of excellent expositional prose from *Talion* by Mary Maddox:

Lu barely survived ninth grade. She had nightmares about school. In them she stood at the brink of two corridors, scuffed linoleum floors and banks of gray metal lockers stretching off forever in mirror images of each other. The odors of dust and floor wax and sweaty gym socks drifted back to her. If she chose the right corridor, she would make it through the day without being hassled. In these dreams she agonized over her choice, knowing it didn't matter, that she was doomed to make the wrong one every time.

Contrast this with the same paragraph written using some of the elements of passive writing that I suggest avoiding—unnecessary adverbs, over writing, and passive verb use:

Lu had barely survived ninth grade. She had so many horrible nightmares about school where she was standing morosely between two corridors that had scuffed linoleum floors with banks of gray metal lockers stretching off forever in mirror images of each other in both directions. She could smell dust and floor wax and sweaty gym socks drifting back to her from along the corridor somewhere. She knew she had to choose the right corridor if she were to make it through the day without being seriously hassled and possibly beaten. In these terrifying dreams she agonized and sweated over her choice, knowing it didn't matter which way she chose, that she would be making the wrong choice every time.

At this stage, you may not see a huge difference between these examples, but hopefully by the end of this book, you'll understand why the first is much better. If you learn how to avoid the elements that make writing passive, then your writing will improve no matter whether you are showing or telling.

What Showing Is

Showing describes what that character sees, hears, does and so on directly, as if the action takes place now, right in front of the reader. It's more immediate and places the reader right in the action. Why try to make our writing immediate? Because it engages readers in a very powerful way.

Telling: Sam was sad.

Showing: Sam's shoulders slumped and his eyes lost their shine.

Here's an example of a shown passage from my book *Prunella Smith: Worlds Within Worlds:*

My feet pounded the hard earth, jarring my bones, but I couldn't stop. The monster closed in behind me, his breath coming in hard, loud pants. I tripped and stumbled over a fallen branch, only just saving myself from a fall. An evil chuckle reverberated through the darkening forest.

'I'm going to get you, bitch.' The chill in the beast's voice sent shivers down my spine.

I ran faster, my legs burning with the effort, and looked desperately for somewhere to hide, somewhere to escape this monster set on destroying the very fabric of my life. But I knew this forest, and knew there was nowhere here that could keep me safe from this thing bent on revenge.

Now take a look at this passive version of the first two sentences: *My feet were pounding the hard earth, jarring my bones, but I couldn't stop. The monster was closing in behind me; his breath was coming in hard, loud pants.*

The telling version of this might be something like: *I ran through the forest looking for somewhere to hide with the beast crashing through the undergrowth behind me. He left a trail of evil chuckles in his wake as if he knew what I knew—there was nowhere in this forest that could hide me from his revenge.*

The passive telling version might be: *I was running through the forest looking for somewhere to hide and the beast was crashing through the undergrowth behind me. A trail of evil chuckles was left in his wake as if he knew what I knew—there was nowhere in this forest that could hide me from his revenge.*

Beginning writers mostly tell their stories, and often in a passive way. Learning how to show a story in an active way takes a bit of study and practice. The rest of this book will help you along that path.

Is Telling Wrong?

The 'show, don't tell' instruction/advice has, for some, become a rule, and wherever they see writing that is somewhat expositional, they scream BAD. What they forget or never realised is that expositional writing has a place in fiction and is, to some extent, a matter of style and personal choice. It is also a matter of fashion. The emphasis on showing rather than telling in fiction came from modern America and has been picked up by Australia and other countries. As I understand it, the advice about showing rather than telling began with Chekhov and the ways he found for implying emotions rather than stating them. TS Eliot was influential along similar lines, with his 'objective correlative', and possibly the spread of creative writing programs in schools and universities has contributed to these ideas becoming the prevailing fashion. British and European writers will tell you that it is less of an issue there, and it wasn't an issue at all until this century—take a look at the classics and books published last century.

Telling is also a necessary shortcut for linking scenes and brief inserts of back-story—just don't write all your scenes as shortcuts or let your back-story languish in huge chunks.

Why then are writing gurus always telling authors to show rather than tell? Two reasons come to mind: It's harder to hold the attention of modern readers who, since they are used to watching movies, require more immediacy to keep them engaged than readers of the past. Also, it's harder to write good fiction in an expositional style because it requires an understanding of rhetoric that goes beyond describing in detail what happens. To tell effectively, the writer must weave descriptive details and imagery into a narrative that may span weeks, months, or even years. In other words, the writer has to be familiar with expository writing, which takes formal education and/or wide reading.

This advice is also given because much modern writing is in first person or third person intimate point of view (POV), which demands immediacy and identification with the character. Without it, writing in those POVs comes off as a little flat. But omniscient point of view and telling a story go together. This is because omniscient POV is written from the perspective of a narrator who stands outside the story and knows everything. So we should expect more telling in an omniscient POV novel along with a sense of the narrator's presence. We can also expect that the narrator will tell us about more than one character's thoughts and emotions, and in a true omniscient POV novel that is not head-hopping. In third person intimate, distance from the characters is a drawback and the author's presence an intrusion; in omniscient POV, distance from the characters and a degree of author presence comes with the territory. (Writing well in omniscient POV is a lot harder than most people think.)

The criteria in the Awesome Indies for 'showing rather than telling' has the proviso of 'where relevant', and this is because a talented author can 'tell' a story brilliantly. In such cases their prose is so good that whether it's shown or told is irrelevant. The task of the critic is to recognise where that is the case rather than see exposition and immediately think 'bad'.

Expositional writing is only 'bad' when it isn't done well, and most of what I see in self-published books isn't. If you want to write fiction that competes well against other books on the market and engages the widest possible number of readers, then—no matter whether you call it genre or literary fiction—unless you really know what you're doing, it's best to follow the general advice to show rather than tell.

The task of modern authors is to learn how to recognise when their prose is passive or expository, learn how to write active prose, and know when it's appropriate to use each one.

Mary Maddox, one of the Awesome Indies reviewers, told me: "I leaned the 'show, don't tell' rule in high school. Since then, I've figured out that both showing and telling are necessary to storytelling. Dramatic scenes usually include some telling, and expository narration and extended transitions nearly always contain elements of showing."

Take a look at the famous opening of *A Tale of Two Cities*. Dickens' opening establishes the wide scope of the novel and introduces an omniscient narrator who will be commenting on events, but having done so, he must move into the narrative, a transition from abstract to concrete. He does this elegantly using imagery structured with repetition and contrast describing the kings and queens of France and England.

It was the best of times, it was the worst of times, it was the age of wisdom, it was the age of foolishness, it was the epoch of belief, it was the epoch of incredulity, it was the season of Light, it was the season of Darkness, it was the spring of hope, it was the winter of despair, we had everything before us, we had nothing before us, we were all going direct to Heaven, we were all going direct the other way—in short, the period was so far like the present period, that some of its noisiest authorities insisted on its being received, for good or for evil, in the superlative degree of comparison only.

There were a king with a large jaw and a queen with a plain face, on the throne of England; there were a king with a large jaw and a queen with a fair face, on the throne of France. In both countries it was clearer than crystal to the lords of the State preserves of loaves and fishes, that things in general were settled for ever.

Later in this book, I (and many other writing coaches) recommend not using phrases such as 'it was' and 'there were', particularly at the beginning of sentences, but here, the usage works and the repetition is powerful. The repetition I'll later advise you to avoid is the unnecessary, cluttering kind, not the kind done for conscious emphasis as it is here. This is an excellent example of why we shouldn't get rigid and emotional about guidelines; what we should do is learn the guidelines and the reasons for them so we know when they aren't relevant. The saying that you must know the rules in order to break them effectively is very true.

Think in Scenes

One way to help you show rather than tell is to think of your book as a series of scenes, like a movie. Pull out the pivotal ones and make sure you write them in an active way, as if they are happening in front of the reader's eyes, not as if you are telling someone the story afterwards. Report what you see, smell, and hear in the scene, as if you're the movie camera. Between the major scenes, you can have some expositional writing, but break up the telling with scenes where you show the action. When we tell the reader about people and events, they don't care that much about them. If you show, they get involved and start to care, because showing is more engaging.

Make sure that you set each scene in a place so the reader can visualise the setting, and use odours, tactile feelings, sounds, and tastes as well as sight in your descriptions—these add texture that draws readers into the scenes in such a way that they almost experience them. Just as a movie director will make sure the lighting is right for the mood of a scene, describe the light quality in your scenes. And don't forget that each scene needs its own story arc and tension. If a scene seemed rushed or 'thin' with too little detail and texture, then write more words to draw out the action and suspense.

Also, don't forget that when something happens to a character, or around a character, the character must respond. The reader wants to know how your character felt, and what they did and said in response to the action. It's an important part of character development.

This seems obvious, but beginning writers often forget to show the responses of characters before moving on with the plot.

Write Like a Movie

The potential audience for books have many other—and, for many, easier—ways to entertain themselves. The biggest competition novels have today are movies and television, and this has altered the kind of novels that are most successful in today's market.

Movies are a highly visual, auditory, immediate and immersive medium. These are the qualities that your novel needs in order to hold someone who might otherwise be tempted to watch a movie. The key to writing that way is in the movie approach itself. If you write your novel as if it were a movie, you'll be on the right track from the start.

How?

Don't think about your story, SEE it as a movie. Visualise it—don't forget the lighting effects—and hear it in your mind.

See it as a series of scenes.

Plot your story arc like a screen play.

Immerse yourself in the characters and scenes as you write. Be in the movie. Write what the character hears, sees and feels.

Write as if you are in the scene and it is happening to you and around you now.

Even though in a movie we do watch from outside the characters, it is still an immersive experience for the viewer due to the visual and auditory power of the medium. In order to give the same kind of immersive experience as they get from a movie, you need your readers to identify with the characters, to get inside them and really know and feel for them.

In summary:

Learning the craft of novel writing and the techniques of writing immediate and engaging prose are vital, but imagining your story in a form that is conducive to that kind of writing and organisation can be a big help. Imagine your novel as a movie, be in it as you write, and you're at least half way there. For some, this is a challenge, but it's one worth taking on because it could revolutionise your writing.

Here's an example from *Stalking Shadows*, the second book in my *Diamond Peak* series. When I wrote it, and now when I read it, I see it like a movie in my head:

A ripple spread from the centre of the lake. Kestril cursed under his breath and Ariel shuddered. Nick rowed faster, arms straining as the lean, elegant lines of a giant serpent's head pierced the surface of the lake and swivelled towards them. Ariel stifled a scream. She could feel the serpent's ominous black-eyed gaze boring into them. The Gana's head tilted to one side as if considering whether to bother with them or not, then it began to swim towards them. Its graceful body undulated behind it like the Loch Ness monster.

Nick heaved at the oars, and though they sped through the water, it would never be fast enough. Kestril took his wand from his belt, stared at it for a moment, then took a deep breath and muttered something under his breath. Music flowed from his wand, a fine sweet voice singing a haunting melody. The song flowed over the lake like something tangible, and it seemed as if the water took up the song until the air itself shimmered with its magic.

The huge serpent slowed, but two more heads broke the water, looked around and fixed their piercing gaze on the travellers. After a moment's consideration, all three sped towards them.

I'm not suggesting you all write like me, not at all, just that you imagine yourself in the midst of your story as you write. Be in it and the reader will more likely be in it as well.

See the Difference

An example of a told passage:

The idea was that she would forget Aarod, but as the days passed, his handsome face kept swimming into her mind and the only way she could get it to go away was to remind herself that he was a murderer. When she remembered the last time she'd seen him, she saw Daniel's face on one of the Magan corpses and the man's haunting eyes became her brother's. The sick feeling that accompanied the memory erased most of her longing, but the sickness lessened with time.

On Sunday, Nadima's day off, she hung out at home trying not to wish that she hadn't told him not to see her again. She lay on the couch, aimlessly flicking pages of a novel that paled into insignificance next to the excitement of her life since Aarod had arrived in it.

Here's the same passage shown:

Nadima lay on the couch in the living room, aimlessly flicking pages of a novel that paled into insignificance next to the excitement of her life since Aarod had arrived. Part of her wished she hadn't told him not to see her again because she couldn't stop thinking about him. Now she had a whole Sunday with no work to distract her from the handsome face that kept swimming into her mind. He's a murderer, she reminded herself, remembering the Magan corpses.

One of them suddenly had Daniel's face. The man's haunting eyes were her brother's, and the blood from the dagger wound was Daniel's life force spilt by the murderer they never found. Whenever she thought like that, a sick feeling lodged in her stomach, but it still didn't banish her longing for Aarod.

Do you see the difference? I've written everything into one scene as if it is happening now and applied the elements outlined in the rest of this book.

Descriptions

I often see books that either have too little description or too much, and I suggest that you try to write descriptions as part of your first draft because it's easier to cut description back at the editing stage than to add description in because you may not even notice that it's lacking. Also, if you're writing descriptions, you're more likely to be 'in the scene' as you write.

I mentioned in the *Think in Scenes* section how important it is to set each scene with some description, but that doesn't mean that you start each scene with paragraphs that do nothing other than tell the reader what a place looks like. Check for this and, if you find it, break up the blocks of description by peppering it into the action, or make sure that it's written in such a way that it adds to the characterisation, symbolism and atmosphere of your story.

Don't think of descriptions as something separate from the story. If you stop the action to give a paragraph or more of description, the reader who just wants to know what happens next will be tempted to skip it. Instead, write what the character notices while he or she is engaged in the action.

This example is from *Stalking Shadows*, book two of my *Diamond Peak* series:

Trees straggled along this stretch of the path, sparse crowned eucalypts peppered with the occasional beech. Ariel and Nick crossed a muddy stream on conveniently placed rocks, wound around enormous clumps of granite, and climbed continually on a gentle grade. Ariel glanced back across the open landscape at the Observatory tower fading into the distance and wondered if she'd ever see the delightful Englishman and his manor again. Up ahead, a black line of trees looking suitably gloomy marked the start of the Morbid Forest. Nick set a blistering pace and Ariel's pack soon began to weigh heavily on her back.

I could have just described this scene as if we were standing still looking around, but instead I have Nick and Ariel doing something. They are crossing, winding around, and climbing. Ariel also looks back and wonders something. Also note the words that reflect Ariel's feelings about the landscape—conveniently placed, gentle, suitably gloomy.

The following description of a new character in *Lethal Inheritance* happens while the man—Tynan, the delightful Englishman mentioned above—smiles, peers at his visitors and shakes hands. I describe his clothes, not when we first meet him, but when Ariel fears he might catch her gawking:

The door opened before they knocked, revealing a tall, well-built man, probably in his late forties. He smiled through his trimmed beard, and bright blue eyes peered at them through round wire-framed glasses. Silver lightly streaked his long fair hair tied at the nape of his neck. He reached out a hand graced with large silver rings and shook Nick's hand.

'Welcome. So good to see you again, Nick.' He turned to Ariel and gave a small bow. 'And you must be Ariel, a warm welcome to you too.'

'Thank you.' Ariel shivered. Her lips felt slightly numb. She hoped Tynan hadn't caught her gawking at his long, loose pale lemon shirt and tie-dyed multicoloured trousers.

What a character chooses to notice and how they describe it tell us a lot about them; a cheerful person is more likely to notice the sunshine than the shadows for instance, but when miserable, that same person would be more likely to dwell on the deep shadows in a room. A teen uses different language to an adult, for example, so their words indicate not just what they're seeing, but also how they feel about it. For example, what is a 'stunning Rueben's original' to the adult with the art history background is 'some kind of old picture' to the teen more interested in stealing the flat screen TV. So your descriptions can deepen your characters.

Settings can also be used as symbols for characters, relationships and even plot complications. For example, a woman who keeps repeating the same mistakes or whose life seems to be going nowhere, looks up at the

Ferris wheel in the fair ground and feels like she's on it. You don't have to labour the links, just having them there adds to the depth of the writing. The quality of the light in a scene is important too; the way light falls on a character (sharp or soft), the colour (warm or cold), the general atmosphere of the environment (tense or relaxed), and the time of day all make the writing more evocative.

And don't limit your description to what a character sees, also show what they smell, feel and hear, and even what they taste if it's relevant. However, don't overdo it. The examples I've shown above are not representative of the writing all the way through the books. They are sections where I'm introducing a new scene or character and so some emphasis on description is required. Readers don't need or want a full account. If I described the hands of everyone, every time a character shook hands, it would soon become tedious. Just describe the things that are relevant to the characters and the action. The things they would notice or that are important for the story.

Here is an example of an overwritten description:

She pushed through the creaky gate into a garden of tall shrubs pressed up against the wooden fence on one side and bordered by grass on the other. Terrified of being seen, she dropped onto her hands and knees and scrambled beneath the shrubs. The bark chip mulch pressed painfully into her bare knees and palms, and twigs caught her hair, but she continued crawling until she came to the corner of the fence separating the garden from the party next door, then she pressed her back against the wooden fence and tried to still her heaving chest and convince herself that none of this was real.

What's wrong with this? Nothing when taken out of context, but if it's in the middle of a scene where the character is running from a pursuer and the reader just wants to know if she escapes or not, then it slows the action down. Some authors fall into the trap of writing their whole novel like this, with every action being described in detail, but the effect is not an immersive experience as they probably hoped, but a tedious one— can we just get to the point!

What you need to ask is: is *how* she gets to the place where she rests important in this scene? Or is the important point that she *does* find somewhere to rest? Is the fact that there is grass on one side, a fence on the other and mulch beneath the shrubs important for the story? Does it matter that her hands and knees are sore and twigs grab her hair? Not in the context of the scene in *Lethal Inheritance* that I used for this example. I did consider writing it this way, until I realised that I needed to keep the story moving at this early stage of the book, and that the next part of the story where she watches a demon feeding off the people at the party is much more important and really does need a detailed description. Had such a key scene followed a passage written like this, it may have lost its impact in all the words.

This is how the above scene appears in *Lethal Inheritance*:

She ducked into the shadowy garden next door to the party, flopped to the ground behind the wooden fence and tried to still her heaving chest and convince herself that none of this was real.

This is the same action pared back to its essentials, to only what the reader needs to know. The word 'shadowy' gives the feel of the garden without dwelling on its appearance and layout, something that actually isn't that important. What's important to the character and, therefore, to the reader is that she *'flopped to the ground behind the wooden fence'*, presumably safe for now. Leaving the description sparse means that the next revelation in the story stands out:

She failed. On one count at least. Her breathing slowed, but even after squeezing her eyes shut and opening them again, she still found herself in her pyjamas tucked under a bush in a garden next door to a noisy party. She swatted at a mosquito that buzzed near her ear, and a sting on her bare arm proved she was awake; but what she saw when she looked through a hole in the fence proved that, if this was reality, it had irrevocably changed.

People filled the Thompson's backyard and every one of them glowed with multicoloured light. Clothes, flesh and blood, bones and organs had become ethereal, their solidity overpowered by the light that streamed through their corporeal forms from some internal source. It seemed as if the light was their real body and their physical one a mere illusion.

I mentioned the mosquito because it not only proves she's awake but also represents what she wants to do with the demon pursuing her—swat it away. That detail also creates a pause here—note that the reader now knows that she's 'tucked under a bush in a garden next door to a noisy party' without me having to describe the process of crawling beneath it. She's safe, so now we can take a breath before going on to the next discovery.

This is how we can play with the pacing by the amount of detail we put into our descriptions. Don't bog action scenes down with detailed description and thought processes. At the same time, don't leave either of these things out completely. Each character and each scene needs a description, but the character description can be as simple and integrated into the action as this one from *Stalking Shadows*:

'What business do you have on Lord Carvell's lands?' the brown-haired, leather-clad man, who appeared to be the leader, asked.

And the scene setting can be as integrated into the action as this—also from the same chapter:

When they drew close to the high stone wall of Carvell village, the captain slowed to a trot, then to a walk as they passed through the gate into the village. He led them along narrow cobbled streets past stone houses a great deal more ancient than those at the Observatory. Ariel loved the colour of their pale terracotta roofs and marvelled at how the builders had made the walls by fitting together rocks and stones of all shapes and sizes, like a jigsaw puzzle.

On a micro level, try to write your descriptions without using 'with', 'that' and 'had'. These words aren't very interesting and can make your descriptions clunky and, if overused, amateurish. We can't avoid these words entirely, and to do so would be unnatural and unnecessary. The point is to try not to rely on them. If you try to write descriptions without such words, you'll find your descriptions become more interesting and lively.

Example:

Dull:
Sally was tall and had long, messy blond hair with red streaks.

Lively:
Sally's blond hair, streaked with red, hung in rat tails around her shoulders. She towered over George.

Be Specific

Be specific as much as possible. Vague words that have a variable basis for comparison like 'big', 'huge', 'expensive', 'cheap', 'plain', 'old' and so on mean different things to different people. Expensive to you and expensive to me may be two totally different things. I'd rather have 'a diamond the size of my fist' than 'a massive diamond', or 'a hand-tailored cashmere suit' than 'a really expensive suit'.

Being specific also gives a much clearer visual image to the reader, and that's the whole point of descriptions.

World Building

World building is usually considered to be something only authors of speculative fiction need to concern themselves with, but that isn't true. Historical fiction writers have to build a picture of a world in times gone past, and those writing about a contemporary world, though they have less to build, still need to make sure that the setting, both physical and cultural, rings true.

Whether it's Victorian England, a planet of technologically advanced spiders or a New York ghetto, the language of the characters, their values and the way their world functions around them must be consistent, either with known facts or within the imaginary world.

I've read several historical fiction books that fall down because the characters use noticeably modern language. If you're doing a time travel theme, the traveller from the future would have different speech patterns and values from those around him or her. And if you're writing about impoverished Americans, the world you create will be different than if you're writing about the privileged, even though both take place in America.

The first thing is to be clear on the society's values, religions, environment and history, and in addition for speculative fiction, the laws of physics that govern the world. If magic is possible, for example, how is it done and what are its limitations? If the planet has two suns, what effect does that have on daylight? Would it have a night time at all? These things must be logical and consistent.

For each event that transcends the laws of physics with which we are familiar, you have to ask yourself: if this can happen, then what else can logically happen and do I want that to be able to happen? If James can do magic, we'll assume that he can do it anywhere and anytime unless you provide some parameters. Without limitations, you'll run into problems with believability.

For example, in one of the early drafts of *Lethal Inheritance*, I had a 'noble one' transform into a 'radiant body of light' and rescue the heroine from reeds that were trying to strangle her. My husband read it and pointed out that if someone in a radiant body could have an effect on the physical world then the rest of the story was redundant. Why, he asked, couldn't a noble one just pick her up and fly her to the top of the mountain? Had I left it in, it would have undermined the whole story. I had to change the parameters of the world so that couldn't happen.

The second thing to consider is how and when to impart the information the reader needs to understand and imagine the world. For contemporary and historical fiction, the reader knows enough that they can read on quite happily without you having to lay out all the specifics that you consider important to the story. The details will come out at the appropriate time in the story.

For speculative fiction, it's quite a bit trickier.

Avoid (especially early on in the book):

- info dumps—a paragraph or more that delivers information in an obvious and cumbersome way.

- introducing lots of strange names and species in a short space of time.

- details of a complex system—politics, religion and so on—all laid out in one chunk.

Instead, find a balance between the reader finding out the details as the story progresses and making sure there is sufficient information that they can see what's going on in a physical and cultural setting.

It's not easy to find this balance, especially in your first speculative fiction story, but the question to ask yourself is: what does the reader need to know at this point to make sense of the story? To answer the question properly, you need to step back and pretend that you have never read the book before. Not an easy thing to do! Make sure you ask your beta readers this question too. Also ask them if the world you've created makes sense.

Characters

Good characterisation is vital for the success of a story. You need your readers to relate to your characters, to like them and want them to succeed. Readers should root for your central character, and you need that to happen quickly.

First, make your characters complex. Give them faults, issues or weaknesses. Some people compose a character description before they write their first draft, others just write and the character develops as they proceed. Whichever way you do it, search for their vulnerabilities; we all have them and whenever you expose them in one of your characters, you deepen your portrayal of the character and increase the reader's identification with them. Why? Because it makes the character real.

A word of warning here, though—don't make them unlikeable. A character flaw could be something that makes them whiney or bitchy, but readers hate such characters, so keep these traits for secondary characters. You don't want your characters perfect, but you don't want them to be annoying either. If readers hate your central character, they'll hate your book.

Second, don't tell the reader the history and character of a character when you introduce them. Such info dumps will mark you as an amateur. Let the information that readers really need to know about a character come out at the points where it's relevant as the story unfolds. A sentence or two here and there is much better than a chunk of information in one place.

Also, it's very rare that the reader needs to know everything that you know about a character, so don't feel you have to tell them everything. Readers will infer things about them and their past from conversations, actions and thoughts. You don't have to spell it all out.

And show us the character's qualities, don't tell us about them. Let the reader find out that Joe is a slob by describing the dirty clothes thrown on his bedroom floor. They'll realise that Betty is brave when they see her dive into a flooded stream to rescue a child, and they'll realise that Tom cares for his mother by the things he says to her and the way he reacts to what she says.

Third, give them challenges, both inner and outer. This adds tension, and also gives a chance for readers to see how they react to and overcome these challenges. Don't make things too easy for them.

Fourth, show us what they think and feel about things. We learn about a character by how they react and how they think, and your story needs both aspects to give a reader a deep connection with a character. We need to see their internal challenges and reactions as well as their external ones.

But don't spend pages on inner monologues or character thought processes in an attempt to deepen your characters; a lot of thinking with nothing actually happening can soon become tedious. Instead, pepper your action with the character's internal reactions, but also make sure you don't repeat internally what is actually obvious from the action.

Characterisation is deepened through strong dialogue, particularly the use of subtext, and through writing descriptions from a character's point of view. So don't think of characterisation as something you do separately to the other elements of your story. And remember that your central character should grow or change in some way because of the events in the story; without this kind of character development, a book can seem somewhat pointless.

Dialogue

Everything after this point in this book shouldn't concern you when you write your first draft. When writing that first draft, just write. Don't care about how badly you might be writing. The important thing is to get your ideas down. Don't let these guidelines break your flow. The idea is that you write with your creative mind, then edit with your conceptual mind. Both are important, but creativity must come first. Remember that these are not rules to bind you, they are tools to help you improve your writing at the self-editing stage.

And now to dialogue:

We learn a great deal about characters from how they talk and what they say, and if our dialogue is stilted, unnatural, or incorrectly phrased for the time frame, it can ruin an otherwise good book. Many books about fiction writing go into dialogue in detail, so rather than repeat what others have said, I'll just point out the things that I often see lacking in dialogue in terms of the focus of this book, which is line editing. So when you edit, check the following:

Ground Your Dialogue

Occasional reference to body movement and scene interaction is important in dialogue. Don't have long conversations with no facial expressions, gestures or description of settings.

Without these, characters become disembodied talking heads. Using them grounds your dialogue in the scene and helps character development. It also breaks large areas of one person speaking into more digestible chunks. You can also occasionally use body movement before someone talks to establish who is talking.

Example:

'When are you going to see your father?' Sally asked.

Could be:
Sally took a deep breath. 'When are you going to see your father?'

An example in the following section shows why we need to ground dialogue.

Keep Tags Simple

Stick to simple dialogue tags like 'said', 'asked' and 'replied' with the occasional 'shouted' and 'yelled'. Forget what your primary school teacher may have told you about avoiding using 'said' too often by using alternative words; there are more skilful ways to do that.

One mainstream publisher I did a workshop with said that when she received a manuscript, she opened it at random, and if she found that the author had a high number of tags or had used anything other than 'said', she rejected the manuscript without reading further. Why? She said it indicated that the author didn't know how to write.

Fancy tags are very obvious. 'Said' goes unnoticed. Replacement words, such as 'remarked', 'commanded', 'agreed', 'argued' and so on stick out—my pet hate is 'opined'. Since it's not a word in common use, it jumps right out at you. Fancy tags are distracting; they remind the reader that they're reading and thus take them out of the story, and you don't want that.

Example:

'Get out of here now!' he commanded.

'Get out of here now!' he said.

It's obvious from the exclamation mark and the words themselves that the sentence is a command. The word 'commanded' is unnecessary and cumbersome.

Whatever you're trying to communicate with your fancy tag should be said in the dialogue itself or by the actions and facial expressions of the characters. The way to avoid using too many 'saids' is to avoid using tags altogether.

Cut Unnecessary Tags

Readers must know who is saying what. It's very confusing if you get to the middle of a conversation and can't remember which character is talking, and it's particularly annoying if you have to go back to the last indication to find out. This can happen easily during conversations where one character speaks for a long time and where the character's voices aren't immediately different.

However, your desire to make sure that the reader knows who's speaking shouldn't always result in a dialogue tag.

Cut dialogue tags completely where it's obvious who's speaking or where you have action as well. The action is sufficient to tell the reader who's speaking if you use the character's name or pronoun.

Overwritten:

'We've got to get away,' John said.

'How? We're stuck here," Mary replied.

'I think I know a way,' John said.

'The only way out of this place is past those guards,' Mary said.

'Shut up and follow me,' John said, setting off towards the shed.

'You'd better be right!' Mary retorted and stumbled after him.

Revised:

'We've got to get away,' John said.

'How? We're stuck here," Mary replied.

'I think I know a way.'

Mary shook her head. 'The only way out of this place is past those guards.'

'Shut up and follow me.' John set off towards the shed.

Mary stumbled after him. 'You'd better be right!'

Where you do need a tag in a line of dialogue, insert it as early as possible. This stops the reader having to read to the end of a long sentence to find out who's talking.

Example:

'Yes, I will eat the dog, but not until you whip the cream for dessert,' he said.

'Yes,' he said, 'I will eat the dog, but not until you whip the cream for dessert.'

But do use tags when they're necessary. Just because only two people are speaking doesn't mean that the reader won't forget which voice they're 'listening' to after several exchanges without some indication of who is speaking. Underusing tags is as inadvisable as overusing them.

Take a look at this version of the above example:

'We've got to get away.'

'How? We're stuck here.'

'I think I know a way.'

'The only way out of this place is past those guards.'

'Shut up and follow me.'

'You'd better be right!'

A great deal is missing from this dialogue now. It's ungrounded, related to nothing in the environment, and though he says 'follow me', nothing indicates that he's actually moved.

Try to vary the way in which you tell readers who's speaking. Use tags, actions, gestures and facial expressions, but again, don't overdo it. Where only two people are speaking, an attribution at the end of each character's words is unnecessary and can simply slow the pace down and frustrate readers who just want you to get on with the story. It's all a matter of balance.

Dealing with Information

People don't actually say everything they think. They keep a lot to themselves, but some beginning writers don't understand this important point, and they have their characters spill the entire contents of their mind in a scene. This can easily happen when you have information that you want the reader to know and you've decided to deliver this information in dialogue. No matter how you deliver it, an info dump is always an info dump, and having a character say the information will not disguise that fact unless you break it up as I suggested in the section on grounding your dialogue.

When the point of dialogue is to express information, instead of having one character simply tell the other all the information, have one ask questions of the other, or have them interrupt occasionally or ask for clarification, which then leads the person expounding to go deeper into their topic. This will make it much more natural.

Also consider argument; having one character disagree with the other and the first try to convince them has much more tension and is therefore more interesting than a straight exposition. Perhaps someone is talking about a political situation. Perhaps you want them to give a rundown of the society as part of your world-building—though it's far better to write so the readers can see it for themselves as the action progresses, rather than having to be told. Let's say that character 1 has explained the double dealing of the government to character 2. Rather than having character 2 simply listen passively, put their reaction in to break up the other's monologue.

'That's so two-faced! They shouldn't be allowed to get away with it.'

'What? That's just the way governments are. They always have to juggle factions.'

'Maybe, but they should stick to what they promised, or at least not do a complete shift away from something they said was important.'

'In an ideal world, yes, but in reality, it's just how it is. I'm not saying it's right, I'm just telling you what happened.'

'Okay, fine. Go on, then.'

You could also have the first give incorrect information that the second person could correct.

Consider a situation where one character is telling the other a story in which someone ran over a dog. Character 2 interjects:

'I thought James ran that dog over, not Lilly.'

'How do you know?'

'It was in all the newspapers. I'm pretty sure he was driving and she was just the passenger.'

'Okay, but either way, she was upset and that's why she got into an argument with Bill.'

Adding these kinds of elements will help break up long passages of dialogue and make it much more interesting. It will put life into it.

Also consider carefully whether:

- The reader needs to know all this information, and if they do:

    - whether it needs to all be delivered here;

    - whether any of it can be shown through

description of events as they unfold, which is preferable.

- The character being told needs to know all this information, or might already know it.

Generally the reader needs less information than you think they do, and if a character would already know something, then don't have another character tell them.

Subtext

As I said before, people don't actually say everything they think. In dialogue, less is often more, and is usually more realistic. If you want the reader to know what a character is feeling, you can write the character's thoughts as thoughts, if you're in their POV—they don't have to express them to the other character. Of course, if you're not in the POV of the character whose thoughts you want to communicate, then you don't have the option of writing out their inner thoughts, but in either situation, you can use their expressions, actions and gestures to communicate how they 'really' feel about the conversation.

I say 'how they 'really' feel' because people do sometimes say one thing and think another, but body language can indicate what they really think. Noting this kind of detail creates subtext in the dialogue, and that makes it interesting and real.

When you use a character's tone of voice, facial expressions, actions and word selection (e.g. do they say 'concerned' or 'pissed off'?) to hint at their real thoughts, the other person can also read and react to the body language. This makes much more interesting reading than laying it all out there.

Here's an example of dialogue with subtext from *Lethal Inheritance*. Ariel's mother has a baby wombat in her arms and she's feeding him from a doll's bottle while she paces up and down their living room.

Two red spots, like fiery eyes, penetrated the darkness and raised goose-bumps on Ariel's arms. A very large dog? More likely that stupid kid from down the street with laser pens. But the red spots disappeared too fast for Ariel to be sure she'd even seen them. She leapt up and pulled the curtains. The creepy feeling disappeared, but she'd have words with that kid at the bus stop tomorrow. He had no right skulking about in their garden.

The wombat sucked on in a steady rhythm but Nadima stopped pacing, her knuckles white where she gripped the bottle. Had she sensed something too? 'I think we should leave early,' she said.

'What?' Ariel's spoon stopped an inch from her mouth.

'The camping trip. Let's leave tomorrow morning.' Nadima plonked the now empty bottle on the bench.

Ariel lowered her spoon. 'No way, I've got training after school tomorrow. There's a race coming up, remember? I'm planning to beat Molly Gainsbrough in the eight hundred metres.'

Nadima pursed her lips, hugged the wombat tighter and patted his back. 'You'd win the fencing medal if you went back to it.'

Ariel grimaced. 'Give it up, Mum, I'd rather run than stick a blade in someone.'

Nadima sighed. 'Fine, we'll go Friday.'

'Why?'

'We'll make it a long weekend. We could both do with the extra day.'

Ariel frowned. What was going on? Her mother never let her skip school. But why complain? 'Fine. Where are we going?'

Nadima stared into space and began rocking the wombat like a baby. 'Somewhere new. It's a surprise.'

'New? What's new within a two hundred kilometre radius?'

'You'll see.' Her clipped tone signalled the end of the conversation.

In this excerpt, Ariel's mother indicates that perhaps she knows more than she's letting on. Our clues are:

- *… her knuckles white where she gripped the bottle,* and Ariel's wondering, *Had she sensed something too?*

- *'Let's leave tomorrow morning.' Nadima plonked the now empty bottle on the bench.* She didn't place the bottle, she plonked it, giving a sense that she'd made a firm decision. You could also read a slight sense of frustration in the action. Is this a decision she didn't want to have to make?

- *Nadima pursed her lips.* This tells us that she's not happy with her daughter's focus on the athletics meet;

- *… hugged the wombat tighter and patted his back.* There's a sense here—remember the bottle—that the wombat is a surrogate child, and this action suggests that she fears losing her daughter;

- *Nadima sighed. 'Fine, we'll go Friday.'* The sigh indicates that though she thinks it's a bad idea, this isn't a battle she's prepared to have. This tells us something about her relationship with her daughter;

- *'You'd win the fencing medal if you went back to it.'*
  Ariel grimaced. 'Give it up, Mum, I'd rather run
  than stick a blade in someone.' This is an example of information being hinted at rather than fully explained. Instead of telling the reader somewhere that Ariel used to be pretty good at fencing, this little piece of dialogue suggests it. It also suggests that Ariel had given up and her mother wasn't happy about that. Why? This is a bit of foreshadowing; the fact that it's there indicates that it's important somehow, and that makes the reader wonder why. It adds to the sense of mystery;

- *'Fine. Where are we going?' Nadima stared into space ...* What kind of place when thought of makes you stare into space? This suggests that there's something strange about this place. She also says that it's a secret, which adds to the mystery;

- *... began rocking the wombat like a baby.* Nadima is still holding the wombat and rocking him 'like a baby'. She's holding onto her baby, reinforcing the idea in point 4;

- *'You'll see.' Her clipped tone signalled the end of the conversation.* This reinforces the idea that Nadima knows more than she's telling and that for some reason she isn't ready to tell her daughter. She's cut the conversation short. Ariel, and the reader, will just have to wait.

Readers are not going to analyse your subtext like this, but the information is there nevertheless, and they absorb it as they read. This scene could have taken place with the wombat in his little bed, but I had him in Nadima's arms to create this subtext. Nadima is right to want to hold onto her baby; the rest of the series tells you why.

I have no doubt that there are much better examples of subtext in dialogue, but being my writing, I know it well. The point is, would it be as interesting if:

- Nadima had actually said to her daughter that she senses something outside and that she thinks they should get out of the house in case it is what she thinks it is;

- Ariel had said that was a great idea, instead of trying to convince her mother to stay;

- Nadima had told Ariel where they were going and why it was a bit of a strange place;

- Nadima had told Ariel why she should go back to fencing.

These are all things that we will discover as the story goes on, so there was no need to lay it all out for the reader up front.

So ask yourself what you want your characters to communicate, whether they would actually *say* all that and whether or not some of it can be communicated non-verbally as a subtext.

Write How People Speak

People often talk in short sentences and phrases, rather than in long sentences with big words, so write your dialogue the way they speak. Modern people also use contractions often. They are much more likely to say 'I'm' than 'I am'. Read your dialogue out loud to see if it sounds natural.

If you're writing speculative fiction with different races, it's a good idea to use different speech patterns for the different races. Races may use different words to refer to the same thing, or may have 'sayings' they use often. Perhaps one race tends to ramble on in long sentences and the other tends to speak in a way that is short and to the point. One race could be marked by the fact that they never use contractions.

These elements help to distinguish one character from another, and establish the characteristics of different cultures, thus deepening your world building. However you decide the characters of a particular race or species talk, stick to that in all your dialogue for that species.

If you're writing historical fiction, be sure that your dialogue uses the speech patterns of your chosen era and that you don't refer to things or concepts that have not appeared yet.

Dialect

Famous books have been written with characters speaking exactly as they sound when they speak, so obviously some people have no trouble reading books where the dialogue is written that way. Ai, 'owever, 'ave a bet of trouble wif anyfing written too 'eavily in dialect an ai nah ai'm naht thi ony woan. Since I have a huge number of books to choose from today, I'll simply pass over any with dialogue written this way. It makes a book hard to read.

Even those who're comfortable with dialect, or not bothered by it, will have to stop sometimes and re-read, or read slowly to work out what is being said. Once again, you've made the reader aware that they're reading. Your words have come between them and the story. I also feel that it's a little insulting to the reader to assume that they can't keep the accent in mind without having it laid out explicitly.

So what do you do when you want to show that a person speaks with a thick accent or in a particular dialect? As with many of the things I'll speak about in this book, it's a matter of degree. I, 'owever, don't 'ave trouble wif dialogue written in light dialect, an' I know I'm not the only one. The important point to understand, and the one that causes overwriting if we don't understand it, is that readers don't need everything spelled out. They get it without you labouring the point.

So when you introduce a character, you can say that they have a thick accent and perhaps write it more fully during the first few sentences so readers get the idea. After that, you lighten it up so the dialect doesn't make the reading a chore. Readers will remember their dialect from other cues in the book like the setting, the slang and more specifically whenever another character mentions their accent or misunderstands them because of it.

Example.

Carter frowned. 'What do you mean, 'go around the 'hull'? I don't see any ship.' He glanced at Adele to see if she'd seen it. She shook her head.

'Thuz no shup,' Paul said. 'Ut's a hull, mate, you know … a hull. A small mountain.'

'Small mountain?' Carter couldn't believe it. 'You mean a hill?'

'That's what I said; ay, mate.'

'No, you didn't, you said a hull.' Carter fixed him in the eye, daring him to deny it.

Adele giggled, slapped her hand over her mouth and turned away.

'Pah. You're just mocking my kewe uccunt.'

'Nah,' Carter shook his head, 'you stumped me and me sheila good and proper.'

This actually happened to me when I was visiting New Zealand. I was born there and lived there until I was twenty-four, but the accent of a man who gave me directions was so strong that I truly couldn't understand what he meant by 'hull.' He thought he was saying 'hill', but it sounded like 'hull' to me. He thought he was directing me around a hill, I thought he was directing me around the hull of a ship.

Carter's use of the word 'stumped' (dumbfounded) and 'sheila' (girlfriend—no capitals because it's a slang word for a woman, not an individual woman's name) might give you a clue to his nationality. Kiwis and Aussies like to rib each other over their accents. If you're from any other part of the world, the humour in this example may well escape you.

The point here is that a section that focuses on a character's accent is one way of making it clear how thick an accent is without you having to write it out.

But, of course, if everyone speaks the same way in your book, no one will draw attention to it in that way, so the idea is to write just a few key words in dialect—the ones that people notice most—as I did for Kiwi Paul above.

If you feel the dialect is really important, you can 'thicken' it up again occasionally at a point where the character's accent may naturally become more pronounced—perhaps when they're excited or angry—but think of the reader; don't make reading a chore.

Don't Overuse Expressions and Characters' Names

Check your dialogue for over use of 'well', 'oh', 'right', 'ah' and so on. Use these rarely. Although characters in real life do use 'well' and other such words before they speak, and it's fine to use them occasionally, they aren't necessary in written dialogue and can easily become cumbersome.

Also, don't use character's names often in the dialogue, unless it is for a specific effect. It's rare when speaking in life, and, again, soon becomes cumbersome.

Example:

'How are you this morning, George.'

'I'm well, thank you, Mary.'

'George, I have something to tell you.'

'What is it, Mary?'

3

Cut the Clutter

After looking at the big picture and making the changes required at that level, you can move onto the first stage of line editing, which is succinctly summed up in the term 'Cut the Clutter.'

The Disease of Overwriting

'The writer who breeds more words than he needs, makes reading a chore for the reader who reads.' Dr Seuss.

'Writers we in time call 'great' tend to follow all the rules of good writing. Spare, interesting, easy to read, easy to understand to the point we forget that we are reading.' G J Berger, award-winning author of *South of Burnt Rocks, West of the Moon.*

'Clutter is the disease of American writing. We are a society strangling in unnecessary words, circular constructions, pompous frills, and meaningless jargon.' William

Zinsser in his classic text, *On Writing Well.*

Writing cluttered with extraneous words is called over-writing. Uncluttered writing says clearly what the author is trying to convey, and it gets to the point without bogging the reader down in deadwood that only bores, distracts, or confuses our readers.

When I gained representation for the first novel in my YA series, my agent asked me to cut 18,000 words from it. I thought that meant that I would have to remove part of the story, but she assured me that if I went through and simply cut unnecessary words, I could do it without losing any content and end up with a much improved book. She was right, and I was amazed at how many extraneous words I found.

So the first step in your self-editing should be cutting the clutter. Removing unnecessary words will make your writing tighter and clearer. Often authors say the same thing several different ways, but you don't have to tell the reader anything that is already obvious or will be in the next paragraph.

To the fledgling writer, overwriting may feel rich or poetic—it did to me too when I started out, before my first editor friend set me straight. I have even seen a reviewer of a severely overwritten book call it poetic. Hmm. But it isn't, and we can make sure that our writing does not suffer from this disease by following a simple rule: cut unnecessary words. Cut out any language that is vague, repetitious, or pretentious.

Cut Adverbs

Try to write without adverbs and certainly keep them to a bare minimum. They tell, rather than show. Replace them with one verb that says the same thing, (e.g. instead of saying he 'looked angrily', say 'he glared') or simply delete the adverb. If you've set the situation well before the adverb, they're rarely needed. If they seem necessary, then your writing may be lacking something. Ask yourself how you can write the scene so that the action the adverb describes is obvious without using the adverb.

Example:

Overwritten: *He ran angrily across the lawn.*
Revised: *He stomped across the lawn.*

Stephen King insists that good writing doesn't need adverbs because the reader gets the idea from the active writing of the scene. He says that adverbs indicate lazy writing.

Cut Adjectives

Double adjectives should be the first to go. If you look

at them objectively, you'll often find that one of them is obvious, or that they're saying the same thing in different ways. Sometimes, but rarely, a double adjective is necessary. One example I use in the *Diamond Peak* series is a calm, clear mind. The clarity and the calm are different aspects of the mind state the protagonists must cultivate if they're to defeat the demons. Calm is not enough and neither is clarity, hence I needed the double adjective.

But often we don't need adjectives at all, and prose can easily become bogged down if they're used too liberally. So check each one and ask: why is it there? What does it add?

Overwritten: *The bright, golden sun warmed us.*
Revised: *The bright sun warmed us.* (Suns are golden. Readers know this so you don't need to say it's golden.)

Or, if the brightness isn't particularly important for the story, remove both adjectives and write: *The sun warmed us.*

Or, if the brightness is important, consider whether it might need more explanation to get across what you want to communicate: *Though too bright for our light-starved eyes, the sun warmed us.* Yes, this is more words, but if they're necessary to express what you want to say, then they aren't extraneous. Whether you emphasise a word or use it at all depends on why the word is there. What is its purpose? What are you trying to say?

Overwritten: *The dark night hid the shed from view.*
Revised: *The night hid the shed from view.*

(Nights are always dark, so you don't need to tell us that it's dark.)
Also consider: *The night hid the shed.*
Is 'from view' necessary? The answer will depend on context, but often such phrases can also be cut.

Reduce Long Clauses

Reduce long clauses:

Overwritten: *The cat <u>who was</u> in the backyard was playing with a mouse.*
Revised: *The cat in the backyard was playing with a mouse.*

Reduce Phrases

Reduce phrases to single words where possible:

Overwritten: *The woman <u>at the start of the line</u> tried to climb the fence.*
Revised: *The <u>first</u> woman tried to climb the fence.*

Avoid Empty Openers

Avoid 'There is', 'There are', and 'There were' as sentence openers. 'There' adds nothing to the meaning of a sentence:

Overwritten: _There is_ *a toy in every packet of Weetbix.*
Revised: *A toy is in every packet of Weetbix.*

Overwritten: _There are_ *two dogs in the yard.*
Revised: *Two dogs* are *in the yard.*

Don't Overuse Modifiers

'Very', 'really', 'totally', and other modifiers add little or nothing to the meaning of a sentence.

Overwritten: *When she got home, Janice was very tired and really hungry.*
Revised: *When she got home, Janice was exhausted and hungry.*

Be Precise and Avoid Redundancies

Replace redundancies (phrases that use more words than necessary to make a point, or words that repeat the same idea twice) with precise words. Unnecessary words are those that add nothing (or nothing significant) to the meaning of our writing. They merely distract from our ideas and make reading like pushing your way through a forest, instead of walking on the path.

Common phrases that mean little, if anything:

- all things considered

- as a matter of fact

- as far as I am concerned

- at the end of the day

- at the present time

- due to the fact that

- for the most part

- for the purpose of

- in the event of

- it seems that

Commonly heard redundancies (cut the word in brackets):

- (absolutely) essential

- (advance) planning

- (all-time) record

- (armed) gunman

- (brief) moment

- (completely) annihilate

- descend (down)

- sit (down)

- (entirely) eliminate

- introduced (for the first time)

- (mental) telepathy

- (outside) in the yard

- (temporary) reprieve

Other words and phrases you can usually do without:

- began to

- started to

- would

- should

- in order to

- because of

- caused him/her/it to

- decided to

- Also check if the following are really necessary:

- that

- then

- after a moment

Do you need that preposition?

- stand (up)—one always stands *up*, so there is no need to add it.

- sit (down)

- smile (on his face)

- touched (with his fingers)

- nodded (with his head)

- gave a wink (of the eye)

Frame Your Metaphors

Frame your metaphors in plain writing. Too many metaphors and similes can choke the writing and slow the narrative. It's like placing a lot of artworks in close proximity without frames to set them off; you can't see them properly and your enjoyment of them is compromised.

Example:

The sun gilded the billowing clouds with ribbons of bright gold. Below her, waves thumped against the jagged rocks like a rock band, and cars roared up the road like fire breathing dragons. To her right, emerald green fields spread like velvet over verdant hills, and ill-foreboding crags of black granite reared before the ghostly spires of the mountain in the distance.

There are some lovely metaphors and similes in that passage, but having them all in the same paragraph with no plain writing between them makes reading it a little like wading through honey.

The following is easier to read:

The sun gilded the billowing clouds with ribbons of gold. Below her, waves thumped against the jagged rocks, and cars roared up the road. To her right, emerald fields spread over verdant hills, and ill-foreboding crags of black granite reared before the ghostly spires of the distant mountain.

The lost words add, rather than detract, from the passage.

Don't Try to Impress

Leonardo da Vinci said, '*Simplicity is the ultimate sophistication*', and this is true in writing as in many other disciplines. Aim to say what you want to say as clearly and succinctly as possible. Unnecessary complexity just makes it harder for readers to work out what you're trying to say. So don't use big words or lengthy phrases when a simpler one is clearer or more precise. It isn't impressive; it's clumsy. Find the best words for the job.

Overwritten: *Doctors who are participating in the conference should be empowered to participate in the food selection process.*
Revised: *The doctors should be able to choose their own food.*

Don't Say the Same Thing Twice

Don't restate something that is already clear.

Overwritten: *"What? I don't understand?" George said, confused.*

Revised: *"What? I don't understand?" George said.* (It's clear from his speech that he's confused, so you don't need to say it.)

Overwritten: *The sun set, sinking behind the hills.*
Revised: *The sun sank behind the hills.*

Also check that you haven't repeated the same idea in different ways in consecutive paragraphs.

Check Back-story

A good general rule is no more than one paragraph of back-story at a time; at the most, two. Otherwise, it can turn into what's called an info dump—an obvious dumping of information. Information and back-story naturally tends to be told rather than shown, so your readers' engagement level can drop if you have too much of it in one place. Readers tend to want to skip big chunks of back-story or information and get on with the present story, so you need to handle these elements skilfully.

First, decide what is really necessary for the reader to know, then put those points into the story at the place where the reader needs to know as single sentences or paragraphs within the action, rather than placing all the information or back-story in big chunks. Authors know everything about their characters, but the readers don't need to know everything that the author knows; a mere hint at something is often sufficient for them to get the idea. Readers can assume one thing from another, and explaining everything in great detail is not only unnecessary but also can be an insult to their intelligence.

That two people meeting have a shared history can be hinted at through their facial expressions, the tone of their voices, and veiled references to the past. Parts of what happened between them can be revealed at various times and the readers can piece the story together for themselves. Not delivering it all as one chunk makes a mystery out of it. The reader wonders what their history is and finds fragments of the answer interesting, whereas if you simply tell them everything up front before it has become relevant and before they've had a chance to wonder, it's unlikely to be as interesting.

This doesn't mean that whole chapters can't be about the past, they can; they just need to be relevant to the main story, written in an engaging fashion and have sufficient dramatic tension to hold a reader. As always, these are guidelines, not rules. But be careful where you place the back-story—it's not a good idea to stop for back-story in the middle of a battle, for instance. That will only frustrate the reader who wants to know the outcome of the battle. Wait until after the battle.

4

Activate Your Prose

After you've cut the clutter from your writing, take a look at the actual prose—the words you've used and how you've used them. This is the level that is often overlooked, but it's the level that makes a big difference in how professional your writing looks, and, in particular, how immediate and engaging the prose is. The less action-orientated your book is, the more important your prose is in keeping readers engaged.

'To be' Verbs

The verb 'to be' and all its variations (be, am, are, is, being, was, were, been) are known as passive verbs. They are general verbs, and rather bland compared to the more specific options that can often be used in their stead. Prose with a lot of such verbs lacks immediacy and is less engaging than prose that uses more active verbs. 'Was' and 'were' are the main ones writers overuse. Your prose will improve if you replace them with a specific, active verb, or restructure the sentence to avoid them.

Examples:

He was after her like a shot. (Passive.)

He raced after her like a shot. (Active.)

She was at the lookout, staring over the railing. (Passive.)

She stood at the lookout, staring over the railing. (Active.)

Their toes were numb with cold. (Passive.)

The cold numbed their toes. (Active.)

When I'm self-editing, I search for all those 'was'es and 'were's and see if I can write the sentences better without them. I usually can. This one tip made a huge difference to the quality of my prose.

The More Evil 'was ... ing'.

Using 'was' or 'were' or 'is' or any other version of the verb 'to be' along with a participle ending in 'ing' is very passive where there are better alternatives. Replace these forms with a more active verb, or see how your sentence reads if you restructure the sentence to avoid it. Often it's just a matter of replacing the 'ing' ending participle with an 'ed' ending one. The 'ed' verb forms are more immediate than the 'ing' ending forms.

Examples:

She was running along the road.

She ran along the road.

They were coughing up blood.

They coughed up blood.

He was skipping towards the car with Jacob's hand in his.

He skipped towards the car with Jacob's hand in his.

If it was important that the skipping occurred at the time of a character's observation of the event, you would leave it as 'was skipping', as in the following: *She turned to the sound of feet on pavement. He was skipping towards the car with Jacob's hand in his.*

'ing' and 'ed'

'ing' ending verbs diminish the action, which is fine when the action is subsidiary to the main action, but it's not good usage for the main action in a sentence. Make sure the most important action has an 'ed' ending. Such words are much stronger and more active, so change 'ing's to 'ed's where you can. Try not to use more than one 'ing' ending word in any one sentence or your prose will quickly lose its impact. In summary: use 'ed' endings for primary actions and 'ing' endings only for subsidiary actions.

Compare:

'Enough play,' the demon growled, glaring at Nick, his mouth dripping green flames.

With:

'Enough play!' The demon glared at Nick. Green flames dripped from its mouth.

'ing' Starting Sentences

Avoid beginning a sentence with an 'ing' ending participle phrase.

Example:

Running through the trees, she shouted for help.

Although this can be effective occasionally (once per 10,000 words is a good guideline), excessive repetition can make your prose flat and 'samey', and at the very least lacking in sophistication. It's often awkward as well. It gives the impression that the author is trying to do something different, and that's the problem—it's noticeable. In good writing, we don't notice the words.

Try restructuring sentences to avoid this construction. Remember also that whatever action you assign an 'ing' ending to is a subsidiary action and that when you use this kind of construction the two actions must be simultaneous, as in the running and shouting in the example above.

In the chapter on sophistication in the book *Self-Editing for Fiction Writers, Second Edition: How to Edit Yourself Into Print* by Renni Brown & David King,, on page 193 they say that this construction is a mark of a 'hack' writer. (Ouch.)

Apparently, some people suggest that this advice is not relevant today, but just as a lot of people stealing doesn't make stealing acceptable practice, the existence of many books displaying this problem doesn't make it good writing. These writers simply aren't aware how it weakens their writing—and why risk being thought of as a hack writer when you have so many other options for sentence constructions?

Unfortunately, even experienced and successful indie authors can make this mistake simply because no one has made them aware of it—or they have ignored the advice—and the more who do it, the more people think it's okay—it really isn't. Ignore this advice and some people will discard your work as amateurish. You'll never know because they won't tell you; they're too busy editing books, teaching their creative writing students or reading better quality books.

Beware of those who reject advice, such as this, that has come from those who have worked as editors for big publishing houses for years, because their arguments often come from defensiveness. "I'm an indie—I can do what I like," they say, and that's fine, if you don't care that you look like an untrained dancer trying to dance ballet. The fact that many of those watching won't notice that you aren't pointing your toes doesn't make it good dance.

If you think this partial ban on 'ing' ending participles heading up sentences is a matter of stylistic choice that you can afford to ignore, show me a book published by the Big Six that overuses this construction, and ask yourself if doggedly holding onto a few dubious sentence constructions isn't more a matter of ego than writing practice.

Besides, how often do sentences starting with a verb ending in 'ing' actually sound good?

Does this really sound better?

Running down the road, she got hit by a car. Thinking quickly, and rolling out of the way of oncoming traffic, she ended up in the gutter but still alive.

Than this?

She ran down the road, but a car hit her. Quick thinking saved her. She rolled out of the way of oncoming traffic and ended up in the gutter but still alive.

And so far, I've only talked about the grammatically correct version. Don't let your participle dangle. When you do use a participle phrase, make sure that it is connected to a human agency. The word after the comma, should refer to a human, not an object.

Wrong: *Having been named chairman, the meeting was called by Craig.*

This is called a dangling participle because the participle is not attached to a human agency. Craig was named chairman, not the meeting.

Correct: *Having been named chairman, Craig called the meeting.*

'There Was', 'It Was'

Using forms of the 'to be' verb after 'it', 'there', 'this' and 'that' is best avoided, especially at the beginning of a sentence. They are unspecific and therefore rather dull words and are usually unnecessary, which means if you're using them a lot, you're overwriting. When added to the problems with using the 'to be' verbs, their use makes for particularly uninteresting writing. Only use these terms if it's necessary for the character's voice, or for some stylistic purpose.

Try writing the sentence without this construction and see if it becomes sleeker and more interesting. It will.

Example:

There was something about her that made him stay quiet.

Something about her made him stay quiet.

'As'

Cut back the 'as he' or 'as she' constructs. They weaken the writing by making one of the actions subservient to and therefore less important than the other. (That's why it's called a subordinate clause.) Replace the subordinating conjunction 'as' with a coordinating conjunction such as 'and' you'll have two independent clauses of equal strength.

'As' at the beginning of a sentence is particularly best avoided if you want immediate writing because it's a periodic sentence—the reader has to wait until the end of the sentence to find out what's happening. It puts a delay before the action, and focuses on that rather than on the action itself.

Example:

Compare:

As he'd heard about the coming rain, John turned off the sprinkler.

With:

John turned off the sprinkler as he'd heard about the coming rain.

And:

John heard about the coming rain and turned off the sprinkler.

The last version gives emphasis to the fact that rain was coming, instead of making it of secondary importance as the other constructions do.

'Could' and 'Would'

Words like 'could' and 'would' are often unnecessary, and in some instances put distance between the reader and the character. They also delay the action, so it's not as immediate. Locate these in your writing and see how your sentences read without them.

Example:

Whenever he saw her walk down the street, he would run out to play with her.

Whenever he saw her walk down the street, he ran out to play with her.

In British English, 'can' or 'could' are often used with verbs of perception such as 'see', 'hear', 'taste', 'feel', 'smell', (e.g. *She could smell his shampoo*). Though this is common usage, the 'could' is not actually necessary, and American English will often use these verbs independently of 'can' or 'could' (e.g. *She smelled his shampoo*). As in many cases where conventions differ, Australian English uses either.

The Unnecessary 'to'

You don't need to tell us what a character is going to do, or why they are going to do it—as in 'in order to'. Just have them do it. The writing and characterisation should be clear enough to indicate motivation without you telling the reader they went 'to' do something. Such usage is another mark of overwriting.

Example:

He turned to go back the other way.

He turned back.

Or:

He turned back the other way.

'Started to' and 'Began to'

The words 'began to', 'started to' and 'attempted to' and so on delay the action, making it less immediate. Just have your characters do it. 'Started' and 'began' are often simply unnecessary. They're a mark of overwriting. Try leaving them out.

Example:

Mary began to skip down the block.

Mary skipped down the block.

Don't Overuse 'Looks'

Don't rely too much on 'looked', as in, 'he looked angry' or 'she looked beautiful'. Instead of writing that something looks beautiful, gorgeous, handsome, horrible and so on, try describing the object so the reader can make that call themselves.

Try writing the description without using the word 'looked'. Describe the action or expression or physical characteristic that makes you think someone 'looks angry'—they may be stamping their feet—or 'looks beautiful'—they may have long golden hair and sparkling blue eyes.

Compare the following:

Walnut looked thoughtful.

Walnut frowned and shook his head.

Of course, like all the other things I'm talking about, it's not wrong to use 'looked'; sometimes it's more natural to do so when in a character's voice, but don't use it all the time. It's a lazy way of writing.

'Heard', 'Saw', 'Knew' and 'Felt'

Using she or he 'heard'/'saw'/'knew' or 'felt' removes the reader from the scene. It reminds them that they're reading about someone. If you describe what a character actually hears, sees, knows or feels without saying that they hear, see, know or feel it, you draw the reader into the scene more. This makes them identify more strongly with the character, making the writing more engaging. Sometimes it is necessary to write this way, but don't use it all the time. Consider how the sentence would sound without it.

Compare:

She peered over the rock and saw that the area was swarming with demons.

With:

She peered over the rock. The area swarmed with demons.

'When' at the Start of a Sentence

Using 'when' at the start of a sentence isn't bad; it sounds fine and you'll want to use it sometimes, but you need to be aware that it delays the action and makes it less immediate, so don't use it a lot where you want exciting writing. Sentences are more active with the subject at the start.

Example:

When they reached the high road, they took a right turn.

They reached the high road and took a right turn.

Put the Action in Order

Where immediacy is important, write whatever happens first, first, otherwise you're taking the reader forward then back again. You don't want anything to stop the onward flow.

Example:

After arriving at the village, they ordered dinner before heading off to bed.

That isn't bad writing, but see how we go from after an event to before one, and we're never in the same time frame as the event. If we want to keep a tight hold on our reader's attention, this might be a better option:

They arrived in the village, ordered dinner, then headed off to bed.

Both are fine, one is just more immediate.

Watch Those Eyes

Do eyes dart all over the place and follow people, or is it a character's gaze that does the darting and following? Be careful here; it's easy to inadvertently give the impression that a character's eyes have jumped out of their sockets and 'roamed' the countryside, or 'jumped' from one person to another. Scanned is a suitable replacement, as in 'James scanned the country-side' instead of 'James's eyes roamed the countryside', and 'gaze' is a safer word to use than 'eyes' when you're referring to where a character is looking.

Also watch that you haven't overused eye rolls. Do a search for 'rolled', as in 'she/he rolled his eyes', and note the page numbers where you find them. Make sure there's a good number of pages between each usage. Rolling eyes can drive some readers crazy. Do the same with the word 'heart' to make sure your characters don't have over-active hearts that do an awful lot of pounding, thumping, fluttering, lifting, dropping and so on. 'Stomach' is another good one to check if you're inclined to write that characters' stomachs flutter, churn, clench and so on. More of this is acceptable in romance and YA, but still make sure you've got plenty of pages between usages.

Some people also say that jaws shouldn't drop, and people can't growl or hiss when they're speaking, as in, "Get out of here," he growled. Others accept such things—I do. I consider that my jaw drops when I'm surprised and that people can speak in a growl, though, strictly speaking, you can't hiss and speak at the same time.

Whether these sort of usages are acceptable or are overused or not is a subjective area, but readers do have pet hates, and it's important to be aware of them so that you don't write something really ridiculous.

I read something like this once: *George threw his eyes out the window, searching for his dog as they drove along.*

I guessed he would have been blind after that.

Vary Your Sentence Structures

Many consecutive sentences that have the same construction make for dull reading. Make some short, some long, some complex, some simple and so on. To vary them, you can combine sentences or cut them in two, or shift phrases around in the sentence. In particular, don't start more than a couple of sentences in a row with a character name or pronoun like 'he', 'she', 'I' or 'they.'

Don't worry about this when you're writing your first draft, of course. Don't break your flow trying to vary your sentence structure. At that stage, just write. Look at this at the editing stage when you read your work aloud. If the rhythm doesn't vary, then vary your sentence construction.

Sentences can be:

Simple: a single clause with one finite verb—a clause contains a subject (noun or pronoun and its modifiers

—what is being talked about) and predicate (a complete verb form and its modifiers—what is being said about it). E.g. *Sam ate the cherry.*

Complex: more than one clause. E.g. *Sam ate the cherry and Joan drank the wine.*

Compound: one main clause (stands alone with a complete meaning) with one or more subordinate clauses (that don't make complete sense on their own). E.g. *Sam ate the cherry, which was somewhat bruised after the beating he'd given it.*

Compound complex: two or more coordinating main clauses plus at least one subordinate clause. E.g. *Sam ate the cherry, which was somewhat bruised after the beating he'd given it, and Joan drank the wine.*

Sentences can also be described as:

Loose: the main idea is expressed first and other elements are added on. E.g. *The teacher destroyed the tests after someone displayed the questions online.*

Periodic: saves the main idea until the end. Used too often, this can annoy readers because they have to read to the end to find out the main point, e.g. *After someone displayed the questions online, the teacher destroyed the tests.*

Balanced: a balanced parallel construction, e.g. *Give me liberty or give me death.* Such sentences are great for making a strong emphasis but should be used sparingly.

Hypotactic: the various elements within the sentence are joined by subordinating and coordinating conjunctions. This produces a smooth, free-flowing effect, e.g. *She twirled around with her hands in the air because she knew she had nothing to fear.*

Paratactic: the links are left out and punctuation marks suffice. This gives an more emphatic, jerky impression. *She twirled around with her hands in the air—she knew she had nothing to fear.*

Sentences can also be unthemetised in that it follows the basic subject, verb, object format, e.g. *She ate too much at the party last night.* Or they can be themetised, meaning that they vary from the above structure. The different options allow you to emphasise different aspects of the sentence.

For example:

At the party last night, she ate too much.

Last night at the party, she ate too much.

Last night, she ate too much at the party.

What she did at the party was eat too much.

Sentences can also be one word (elliptical), e.g. *Help.* The rest of the sentence is unwritten but is understood from the context, i.e. *Will you help me?* Single word sentences are useful in dialogue because we often speak this way, and can be used for emphasis in fiction. But be careful not to overuse them.

The Result of Applying These Principles

The following paragraph is typical passive writing in a description. It may sound fine to some of you, but it can be a lot better. These days, I can't bear to read this kind of writing for long, yet I wrote this years ago, before I did any writing study. I thought it was pretty good at the time!

The dragons were the size of semi-trailer trucks and with iridescent scales were as beautiful as they were fearsome. Their limbs were short and muscular with claws the length of long swords, and their powerful tails had spikes along their ridges and a mean-looking barb on the end. Their enormous semi-transparent wings, powered by strong muscles, looked misleadingly delicate, but the fine fabric was much tougher than it looked.

What's wrong with it and how do we make it better?

This is where knowledge of the craft of writing becomes really helpful. Your study will let you identify the weaknesses and show you how to improve the passage.

Let's apply what we've learnt:

*The dragons **were*** [avoid using forms of the verb 'to

be'] *the size of semi-trailer trucks and,* **with** [avoid 'with' and 'had' in decriptions,] *iridescent scales,* **were** ['to be' verb] *as* **beautiful** *as they were fearsome.* [telling the reader they're beautiful rather than showing them what makes them beautiful so the reader can see for themselves]. *Their limbs* **were** ['to be' verb] *short and muscular with claws the length of* **long** *swords,* [unnecessary adjective—swords are long] *and their* **powerful** [it would be better to show the tail's power in an action sequence rather than tell the reader with this adjective] *tails had spikes along their ridges and a mean-looking barb on the end. Their enormous semi-transparent wings, powered by strong muscles,* **looked** [don't rely on 'looks'] misleadingly delicate, but the fine fabric **was much tougher than it looked**. [How does the narrator know this? Better to show its toughness in action.]

Now we know what has to be changed, we can find a more immediate way of saying the same thing. Here's an improved version:

Dragons with short, muscular limbs and claws the length of swords slashed out at each other. Their backbones shimmered with spikes, and their tails ended in lethal barbs. Enormous semi-transparent wings ribbed with fine bones beat the air like drums; tails slapped like iron doors slamming, and thunderous roars reverberated across the landscape.

The golden dragon gleamed like pure burnished gold, and the black scales on his opponent shimmered with a dusting of metallic blue. They sparkled like jewels on a ballerina's wrist as she twirled in a deadly dance.

5

Clarifying Common Confusions

Another thing to check in your self-editing is that you have a clear understanding of the following often-mis-understood punctuation conventions. Some traditional publishers even get them wrong, so if an editor handles these differently, question it. A publisher can create their own style guide, of course, but they should have a good reason for going against general convention.

Ellipses

Major world style guides agree that ellipses should have a space either side of them ... like that. Apparently some UK English style guides suggest a space only at the side where the words trail off... like that, but I have never heard of a style guide that accepts no spaces around ellipses.

Em Dashes

Em dashes are double the length of a hyphen—like this. Traditionally, they have one quarter of a space either side in printed books. However, word processing software doesn't allow us to create one quarter spaces, so the general recommendation for authors is not to use any gaps on either side. Online, however, we can't do that. When we hit a dash twice and press enter, we get two dashes, not the em dash we get in word processing software. Because of this, when writing online we use a space, a hyphen and another space in lieu of a proper em dash. This causes confusion as to what is correct in books. People assume that because that's how we see it online, it's okay like that in books. Perhaps one day it will be, but in the meantime, it's preferable in ebooks we offer for sale to stick to the proper em dash length and use no space either side.

In paperbacks, if you or your formatter uses InDesign software and can manage the one quarter space either side, then do so, if not, go for no spaces.

Introductory Phrases

All style guides agree that introductory phrases should have a comma after them if they are longer than about five words. When we write something like this we have written an introductory phrase. When we read the previous sentence, we have to pause and take a breath after 'this'. That's a clue that there should be a comma there. Now see how much easier it is to read it with the correct punctuation: When we write something like this, we have written an introductory phrase.

Formatting

Fiction should be formatted with a first line indent and no gaps between paragraphs. The first paragraph of a chapter, however, has no indent. This is important in print books, but is not so crucial in ebooks.

Non-fiction has spaces between paragraphs and no first line indents.

Choose one or the other style and stick to it throughout the book; don't mix them together unless you require special formatting, perhaps for poetry, excerpts or quotes.

UK and US Differences

This is a general summary of the main differences between British and American English. This is not a comprehensive list. I give this for those of you who may inadvertently criticise something in a book written to a different set of conventions than those with which you are familiar. They aren't wrong; they're just different.

Grammar

Simple past vs present perfect tense:

Speakers of American English generally use the present perfect tense (have/has plus past participle) far less than speakers of British English. In spoken American English it is very common to use the simple past tense as an alternative in situations where the present perfect would usually have been used in British English.

Example:

Did you read that book?

USA: *No, I didn't read it.*

UK: *No, I haven't read it.*

Verb agreement with collective nouns:

In British English, collective nouns, (e.g. staff, government, class, team) can be followed by a singular or plural verb depending on whether the group is thought of as one idea, or as many individuals.

Example:

My team is winning.

The other team are all sitting down.

In American English, collective nouns are *always* followed by a singular verb, so an American would usually say:

Which team is losing?

Whereas in British English both plural and singular forms of the verb are possible, as in:

Which team is/are losing?

Past Tense forms:

Some verbs (e.g. learn, smell, get, saw) have different simple past and past participle forms in American and British English. The irregular past forms burnt, dreamt and spoilt are possible in American English, but less common than the forms ending in -ed.

Example:

British speaker can say *'learned'* or *'learnt'*, but American speakers would only use *'learned'*.

Punctuation

Mr., Mrs., and Ms. all take periods in American English. In British English, the periods are omitted, following the rule that a full stop/period is used only when the last letter of the abbreviation is not the last letter of the complete word. Unit symbols such as *kg* and *Hz* are never punctuated.

Dates: The order and punctuation of dates is different. British usage omits the apostrophe in the plural form of dates (e.g., 1980s), whereas the American practice more often includes it (e.g., 1980's). The British style is becoming more popular in America, however.

American usage puts the month first, followed by the day, and then the year. Hence, 12/5/2010 means December 5, 2010, in American usage. The British practice (followed in most of the world) is to put the day first, followed by the month. Hence, 12/5/2010 means May 12, 2010, in British usage. The International Organization for Standardization (ISO) has established the YYYY-MM-DD format, in which December 5, 2010, would be written 2010-12-05.

Quotation Marks: British English uses single quotations, American uses doubles.

American style places commas and periods inside the quotation marks, even if they are not in the original material. In the British style, punctuation is only placed within the quotation marks if it is punctuation that is a part of, or is related to, the quoted text.

Example:
A sign on the front door announced that the owners were "out to lunch." (American)
A sign on the front door announced that the owners were 'out to lunch'. (British)

The serial comma: This is used in the USA but rarely in UK English.

Example:
"The cat, dog, and the mouse." (American)
"The cat, dog and the mouse." (British)

Comma usage after abbreviations i.e. and e.g.
US: i.e., what George said, or i.e.; what George said.
UK: i.e. what George said.

Spelling

Words ending in IOUR have been changed to IOR in America (e.g. behaviour).

Many words ending in YSE or ISE have been changed to YZE or IZE in America (e.g. analyse, categorise, standardise). Also YSED or ISED to YZED or IZED, and ISATION to IZATION.

Words ending in RE have been changed to ER in America (e.g. centre, metre).

Words containing the silent letters OUGH have been changed in America so they are spelt phonetically, e.g. doughnut (UK) but donut (US), and hiccough (UK) to hiccup (US).

Words containing a double consonant before ING and ED have been changed to one consonant (e.g. travelling).

6

Choosing an Editor

Once you've worked through your book and edited it according to these principles, you'll have a book that doesn't need as much editing by someone else, at least in the line editing area—I may be doing myself out of a job by publishing this! You'll still need someone else to edit it for you, however, because we can never see our own work the way others do. But if the editor won't have to reconstruct sentences for you, he or she won't need to charge you as much.

So now you're faced with having to find an editor, or perhaps an editing service that uses different editors for the different kinds of editing according to their area of expertise.

What Makes a Good Editor

Norman Podhoretz, editor of *Commentary* magazine, encapsulated the editor's role with this statement: "...

to improve an essentially well-written piece or to turn a clumsily written one into, at the very least, a readable and literate article, and, at the very most, a beautifully shaped and effective essay which remains true to the author's intention, which realizes that intention more fully than he himself was able to do. He cares about the English language; he cares about clarity of thought and grace of expression; he cares about the traditions of discourse and of argument."

Before I began studying writing and editing, I thought that an editor was merely someone who corrected grammar, spelling and punctuation. I thought the job was somewhat dry and prescriptive. There were rules, I thought, that the editor had to make sure were followed so that the grammar and so on was correct. Now I understand that this is only one aspect of editing.

Correcting grammar, punctuation and spelling is the role of the copy editor, but there are other kinds of editing that are just as important in the production of quality writing, and different skills are required for the different areas. A good editor in one area is not necessarily a good editor in all areas, and it takes more than a formal qualification to make a good editor because in all but the copy and proofing, good editing relies on artistry and intuitive understanding of the author's intentions as much as knowledge.

What makes a good structural/developmental editor?

The ability to:

- Pick out the main thrust of a story and know how to pare back what is extraneous;

- See the underlying concepts and know how to strengthen them;

- See what isn't in the book and should or could be;

- Analyse the strength of the various elements of fiction and suggest improvements.

What makes a good line editor?

The ability to:

- Evaluate the details of characters, descriptions, action and timing to remove unnecessary repetition and pick up continuity issues;

- Restructure sentences to vary their constructions, provide aesthetically pleasing rhythms, turn passive into active prose where relevant and so on;

- Pick up unrealistic or stilted dialogue and re-phrase it into something more natural;

- Remove overwriting and generally cut the clutter.

What makes a good copy editor?

Knowledge of grammar, punctuation and spelling, and how to apply them in different circumstances. They should also know the areas in which language is changing and therefore where the 'rules' are somewhat flexible. They should know when it is appropriate to leave poor grammar and spelling in direct speech, as in dialects.

What makes a good proof-reader?

The same knowledge as above plus the ability to focus on each sentence as a separate unit and see what is actually there rather than what we assume is there. A good proof-reader keeps aloof from what he or she is reading. Being swept away by a good story is the prime reason for missing typos. Reading from the back of a book to the beginning is a way to avoid getting caught up in the story and is a recommended proofing practice.

Other important qualities

A good editor also has good people and communication

skills. They know when and how to explain their reasons for suggestions and are encouraging and supportive whilst inspiring the author to stretch their writing to greater heights. They are patient, honest, enthusiastic about your book, can work to deadlines and have no egotistical investment in the work. They assist the author to create the book the author wants to create. They know not only how to retain the author's voice and vision but also how to strengthen it. They don't seek to replace it with their own.

Copy editors and proof-readers primarily require knowledge and precision, whereas developmental and line editors, as well as knowledge, require good analytical and creative problem-solving skills. At the developmental and line editing stages, editing is as much an art as it is a skill.

How do you find a good editor?

To evaluate if an editor is right for you, check their formal qualifications, experience and recommendations from other authors, but also read their blog and what they say about their work process. Reading an editor's blog is a good way to get to know them.

An editor who has reviewed a lot of books in a wide range of genres will have a good understanding of voice and style and how to stay true to it, so take this kind of experience into account.

If you're looking at a team of editors, then look at the person doing the line editing because they're the primary editor in a full editing service. You'll be working most closely with this person, and you need to feel that you can trust them.

Leave a question on their blog. Do they answer you quickly? How do they respond? How do they treat you? Do you think you could work with this person?

Booking a manuscript appraisal is a good (and hopefully cheap) way to start the editing process and see if you can work together. An editor's suggestions in a manuscript appraisal will show whether they're in tune with your vision or not. It will also show you how well they communicate and respond to your concerns. The big question is whether or not the editor understands what you're trying to do. Do they respect your style? The last thing you want is an editor who will try to turn your contemplative romance into a fast paced thriller.

Once you're seriously considering an editorial service, ask for a sample line edit. A sample line edit should include explanations of why the editor has made changes. And if you aren't sure of anything, you should feel free to ask. You can also check things you're not sure of by doing your own research.

If you're happy with the sample edit—and remember that the editor will see things that you don't, so expect to be surprised and educated—and you feel that you can trust the editor to improve your book, not mulch it, then hand it over.

All books benefit from the eyes of a line editor, but the line editor might make some fairly big changes to your sentence and paragraph structure, so it can be a bit scary to hand your book over. It's less threatening to your ego to just have your book copy edited, but a copy edit alone will not make your book better. It will only make it free of grammatical, punctuation and spelling errors, and a book free of such errors is not the same as a good book. A line editor can't make all books great, but they can make most books better.

When you get your book back. Take a deep breath before looking at it, remind yourself that the edits are to make your book better and tell your ego to take a walk. It's time to be objective, not defensive.

Look at the edits objectively. Remember that the editor thinks they have improved your book, and since generally they have more knowledge than you and they definitely have a more objective eye than you, they probably have—unless you've booked someone who isn't really qualified, (avoid big egos, no actual editing qualification, little experience and few recommendations from other authors). If you can't see why something is supposedly better, ask, and research their answer to see if others agree with their perspective. A good editor will leave comments to explain why they've done anything major, anyway.

What they shouldn't have done is change your voice or intention. A skilled line editor can cut words, reorganise paragraphs, combine or cut up sentences, and change your sentence structure without changing your voice. So don't panic when you see that they've done a lot of it. It should strengthen your voice, not weaken it. And it doesn't mean your book was bad, it just means that now it's a lot better.

If your book doesn't need a lot of work, then an editor should be able to do a line and copy edit together, but always—I can't stress this enough—always make sure that a different person does a proof read.

7

Giving and Receiving Feedback

Giving and receiving feedback is part of the job for authors—particularly receiving it—and it's an area that causes a lot of unnecessary pain. A great deal of that pain can be avoided through understanding the following points and through learning how to give and receive feedback in the most beneficial way.

The Necessity of Honest Critical Appraisal and How to Give it

Writers in the online writing community generally give each other a lot of support in the form of knowledge sharing and encouragement. That's great, but sometimes what authors consider support might be a little short-sighted. Does our desire to be supportive mean that we always say something is good, even when it isn't? This may appear to be supportive, but it's not helpful in the long run because honest critical appraisal is a vital ingredient for improvement on both a personal and an industry level. Without genuine feedback on our work, we could think our book is ready to publish when it isn't, and every book published in an unfinished or unedited or poorly conceived state diminishes the status of every self-published work in the minds of readers. This is why self-published books are considered inferior by some. Frankly, a lot of them are, and their authors need honest feedback if they are to improve.

I say authors are 'generally' supportive because bullies and those who like to complain loudly do exist. Reviews are often the stimulus for this kind of behaviour, which is no doubt the reason so many of us are reticent to tell the truth when evaluating others' work. We don't want to upset anyone, so we don't say anything unless we can say something good—fair enough. No one wants a backlash of negative reviews by authors who don't like what we've told them, so we don't risk it.

The downside of not saying anything if we can't say something good, however, is that we have authors who think they are writing great books when they aren't. If no one tells you, then you simply don't realise. We can say that readers won't buy their books so they will get the message that way, but quality is not a guarantee of sales, good salesmanship is. Sales do not equal quality. A lot of indie books have great stories and sell well, but the execution is just a little sloppy. The inadequacies in the writing and editing are not necessarily something an ordinary reader would notice. Many authors think that so long as readers don't notice, or don't mind, it's okay. The trouble with this attitude is that, over time, the quality of written English deteriorates, and though they don't realise it, readers *are* missing out.

So the industry needs genuine critical appraisal, and, as fellow authors, it's best we give it in a polite and respectful way—this is one of the aims of the Awesome Indies. We also need to learn to take it like a professional, even when it's rude. Negative feedback can always be given privately, but published authors must expect the occasional public negative review—it comes with the job. The important thing is not to let it destroy your peace of mind.

Giving good critical feedback is not easy, but with a bit of thought, we can improve our ability to be helpful, and though dancing around people's egos shouldn't be necessary, we can write feedback in a way that will minimise the hurt.

Always point out the good aspects of a work. This isn't just to massage the author's ego, it's because knowing our strengths is as important as knowing our weaknesses.

Don't attack the author as a person—you're evaluating their work, not them—and try not to use inflammatory words.

The most helpful feedback is specific. Something generic like 'it needs work' is not that helpful. And the very best feedback is where the reviewer suggests how something can be improved. They point out the problem, then point out the solution. Writing that kind of feedback takes a lot of time and consideration though. So anyone who gives comprehensive and honest feedback—no matter how negative or how wrong you think it might be—is showing the greatest support. They care enough to give you their time and to risk your being upset with them. That level of care is a rare and beautiful thing.

Not everyone can see the specific problem, however, and even fewer of us can see solutions. These are skills that not everyone has. And that's why hiring at least one professional to critique your work before publication is a good move. Manuscript appraisals do not have to cost the earth—mine don't.

But everyone can be honest and say there is a problem where they see one. Not speaking up is not real support.

I've critiqued several truly substandard books where the author has cited accolades from his or her online critique groups as a reason to discredit and disregard my considered feedback. In all instances, the critique group had given plenty of support, but no real critical appraisal. The result was that these authors published their books in a state that did their writing career no good at all. Perhaps the members of the group simply didn't have the skills and knowledge needed to see the faults—something to be aware of when choosing a group, and another reason to turn to someone with experience in manuscript evaluation.

The least we can do when asked for a review is give our honest opinion. And on the other side of the fence, we must learn to think more of the person who tells us the truth, not less—it takes courage to tell the truth when you risk a backlash. That they're prepared to do that for you shows they care.

If all we give each other is support without the real help of honest critical appraisal, then we could be contributing to ending a potentially beautiful career before it's even begun. Would you rather have false accolades, or real honest feedback that will help improve your work? One feeds our ego, the other feeds our progress as authors.

A Review Structure

My decision several years ago to formally review others' work had a profound effect on my development as an author. Through it, I learned to view my own work in an objective manner, and that ability is a huge bonus for an author. So I recommend that you give it a go even if you don't actually publish the reviews.

To avoid the kinds of difficulties authors can get into when reviewing, I suggest that you make a rule never to review a friend's book—at least not on request. Expectations can ruin friendships, and even those who say they only want an honest review can turn snarky or at least argumentative when your honest review is less than 5 stars.

But how do you go about writing a review?

Answer:
Hook + Summary + Analysis + Closure = Book Review

The hook is a statement, fact, quote, or question that draws readers in and, in a more professional capacity where you're enthusiastic about a book, can potentially give authors a snippet to work with in their promotions.

The summary is a quick summary of the content, preferably without repeating what is readily available in the book blurb.

The analysis analyses the writing itself. It provides a detailed evaluation along with justifying examples. The goal being to touch on at least half of the following: plot, descriptive elements, dialogue, target audience, grammatical and editing elements, characterization, character development, conflict, pacing, prose, flow, and point-of-view.

The closing statement ties everything together. This is also an opportunity to supply one last encouraging push of recommendation or, in some cases, a regretful warning.

Recognising Personal Preferences

There are basically two kinds of reviews. Both are valid, but readers and writers of reviews need to recognise which reviews fall into which category so that we know what a particular review is evaluating. If we're a professional reviewer or book blogger, then we need to make sure that we write fair reviews.

The two main review styles are the 'did I like it' style and the 'is it a good book' style. When these are clear, they are easy to read, but when someone attempts to write an 'is it a good book' review without separating personal preference and objective evaluation of craftsmanship, we get something that is unfair to authors and confusing or misleading for readers.

The 'Did I Like it' Review

This is easy to write; you either like a book or you don't. You're not evaluating how well it's written, you're just saying what you liked and what you didn't. It's good if you can try to find something good to say about a book, but the important thing in this kind of review is to make it clear that it's your personal opinion. On Goodreads you see mostly these kind of reviews, so ratings there are more about how many people liked a book than about the quality of the writing. You can have high rating books that are really badly written, but the reviewers either didn't mention it or didn't realise.

Alternatively, you can have well-crafted, even brilliant, books with low starred reviews simply because they push people's buttons.

If readers see ratings as an indication of quality, then books that are controversial can suffer from the 'did I like it' kind of reviews. The book's overall rating is brought down because readers got offended, or disagreed with the book's underlying philosophy, or found it too dark or too light, or they didn't like the ending, for example. However, if readers check out the low starred reviews, they may find opinions that help them decide to purchase the book.

For example, one person may complain that a book is too Christian, another reader may find that that review confirms that the book is exactly the kind of book they want to read.

So don't assume that a mediocre overall rating indicates a bad book and that a high overall rating indicates a good one.

The 'Is it a Good Book' Review

This kind of review is harder to write. It's the kind of review that professional reviewers write and that authors should be writing about other authors' work. Any review will be subjective to some degree, but to be fair to the author, if we're attempting to say whether a book is good or not, then we must separate our 'likes' from our evaluation of craftsmanship.

Anyone writing this kind of review should have a clear criteria for how they set their stars.

Separating our Preferences from our Evaluation of Craftsmanship

The following aspects of craftsmanship are either right or wrong.

Basic grammar (except in dialogue);

Misuse of words such as *their, there, they're*; *its* and *it's; lightening* and *lightning, effect* and *affect* and so on;

Spelling and punctuation—but you must be aware of the differences between UK/Australian and American English conventions. Also the use of commas can be a stylistic choice. If it's stylistic choice, then usage should be consistent.

These aspects of a novel are either well-crafted or poorly crafted:

- Plot structure—such things as, is there a protagonist and an antagonist? Do the characters have clear goals that are thwarted? Without these, there is no plot. Does the plot wander aimlessly?

- Info dumps—where information is placed in the text in chunks that are not integrated into the story;

- Scenes either move the story forward or they don't;

- Writing quality, e.g. as explained in *Self-editing for Fiction Writers by Renni Browne & Dave King* (passive writing, POV issues, good dialogue etc.);

- Overwriting is always poor craftsmanship, i.e. pages of writing that say the same thing and could be said succinctly in one or two paragraphs;

- Head-hopping in third person intimate is always poor craftsmanship—no, it's not personal preference. Remember the section on point of view?

Although relevant to craftsmanship, our evaluation of the following is subject to personal preference:

- Amount of description;

163

- Character believability, i.e. appropriateness of their motivations and reactions, e.g. what a person of a certain age might do or not do, or say or not say;

- How well we feel we get to know a character;

- Degree of repetition;

- Plot pacing—some people like slow beginnings, others like to jump into the action. Some like a plot never to slow down. Others prefer breaks to take a breath;

- Clumsy phrasing. What you find clumsy may be a common expression in another country;

- How well the ending was tied up;

- The believability of fantasy worlds in speculative fiction;

- Whether there are plot holes or not.

The following are not relevant at all to the quality of the book:

- Handling of the subject matter, e.g. how lightly or darkly the subject is taken, or how deep the perspective is;

- The balance of action, humour, sex, horror etc. in the story;

- Character likeability;

- Our understanding of the book's subject matter or underlying themes (unless it's so poorly expressed that no one could understand it). Our understanding depends on our cultural, philosophical, and scientific knowledge and conditioning;

- Our interest in the subject matter. What you find boring, I may not. What I like, you may not;

- Whether or not we liked where the story went and how it ended. This is the author's choice.

- Style. It's easy to make the mistake of assuming that the author is trying to write the kind of book you would write, so it's good to identify the author's style and see how it differs to how we might treat the same story. What kind of a story is the author trying to write? Is s/he aiming for a gripping sci fi or a more laidback philosophical treatise? We must evaluate their book in terms of what they were trying to do, not in terms of what we would aim for if we were the author.

And the point of all this is . . .

Be clear on what kind of review you are writing. If you're writing the 'is it a good book' review, then make sure it isn't just about the last two categories. You should also consider things in the first two categories and note what is well done, even if you really don't like the book.

You know a good 'is it a good book' reviewer when they can say something like, "Although I didn't personally like some aspects of this book, it's a well written, well thought out book, and those who like [insert relevant preference] would probably love it."

A Beta Reader's Checklist

Here's a checklist you can give beta readers to help them organise their thoughts and focus on the kind of feedback that will be most helpful to you:

Use Track Changes comments to write your thoughts on the manuscript as you read.

Tell me where:

- You particularly enjoy something;

- You lose interest;

- You find something unbelievable;

- You think of something that should have happened and didn't, e.g. a reaction;

- A character does something that seems inconsistent with their character;

- Something seems unnecessary, too obvious to be stated or doesn't lead anywhere;

- There's a plot hole;

- The dialogue sounds wrong or unnatural;

- Anything else comes to mind.

In general, tell me:

- Were the characters complex, well developed, easy to relate to and realistic?

- Is the story interesting?

- Does the book end in a satisfactory way?

- Does the story move at a good pace? Are there places where it lags?

- What do you see as the main issues?

- What suggestions do you have for improvement?

How to Handle Negative Feedback

Truth is essential, but it can also be painful.

It's natural to feel disappointed, even devastated, after critical feedback, but if we can deal with it in a positive way, it can be the best thing for your development as a writer.

For the unseasoned writer, defensiveness kicks in automatically. You take the feedback as personal criticism, and that hurts. Understanding the psychological process that follows from viewing it in this light is the first step towards recognising our reactions and making the decision to look at the whole thing in a more positive, less painful, way.

Shock: You thought your book was pretty good. You've worked so hard on it. It can't be true. They must be wrong.

Defensiveness : You criticise and reject the reviewer and their evaluation. What credentials does the reviewer have, anyway? What do they know? It's only a personal opinion. It doesn't mean anything. You tell yourself this to devalue the criticism. You want to be able to ignore it, so you try to prove that the person doesn't know what he or she is talking about. At this stage you won't see anything worthwhile about the review, even if it's staring you in the face.

Depression: You feel terrible, crushed, even devastated. If they are right (despite trying to dismiss the feedback, part of you says that at least some of it must be true), then you're a terrible writer and you'll never be any good. (They didn't say that; it's what you're reading into it). You feel like giving up.

Letting go: You give up your defensiveness and seek a way out of your depression. You may give up completely for a time, or you forget the book and do something else. You may decide you're never going to write again, or that there are more important things in life and you put your focus elsewhere. This isn't a bad thing. You need to let go to clear your mind so you can start fresh with renewed energy, and giving up is a way to let go, and so is putting your energy and focus elsewhere. I recommend giving up for at least one minute. Totally letting go, even for an instant, is a very refreshing thing to do and it realigns your priorities.

The bare minimum here is letting go of your defensiveness. You have to come to a place where you're prepared to consider that perhaps the reviewer has a point and that rather than rejecting it, you could learn from it.

Objective evaluation: After a break, you come back and look at the feedback in a more objective light. Okay, you think, what is this person actually saying here, and does it apply? If you don't let go, you can't do this. You'll be stuck in defensiveness or depression.

Acceptance: You recognise the value of the feedback and see where it's valid. A professional review (i.e. one that evaluates the craftsmanship of a book, not just whether the reviewer likes it or not) has more value than a reader review for evaluating your craftsmanship. Readers' reviews are the most important thing for indicating potential sales, but not for indicating craftsmanship.

Moving on: You consider how to improve your work in light of the feedback. Then, if you just can't face working on it again, you put the book aside, and focus on improving your next book, or you do the work and improve the book.

Satisfaction/gratitude: You recognise the improvement in the book, or at least in your knowledge, and are glad you went through this process.

How to remove the pain:

What's the trick for dealing with criticism without pain? Cultivate a positive way of thinking about it so you can use the feedback as a way to learn. Consider the following:

Call it feedback, not criticism;

Your integrity as an author is not diminished by a less than perfect book;

No book is perfect;

Most books can be improved;

Your work is not you, so don't take the criticism personally. It's just a book they're talking about;

A review by a publishing industry professional is feedback that will help you improve your work. (I'm talking about constructive criticism on craftsmanship by professional reviewers, not reviews with no basis for their comments apart from the reviewers' dislike);

Recognise the symptoms of defensiveness. Take a deep breath and let it go, so you can go directly to the objective evaluation stage. Drop that defensiveness like a stone thrown into a pool of clear water. Let it sink to the bottom and dissolve.

Does this look familiar to you? Do you automatically become defensive? How able are you to drop it and accept the criticism?

The Good News on Criticism

As well as support, writers need truthful criticism, but even though we may intellectually know that it's a good idea to get good solid criticism, our poor little creative ego still just wants to be stroked and cosseted. Will we ever be able to listen to criticism without a little jab of pain or disappointment or disillusionment or self-doubt?

The good news is that handling criticism gets easier:

- The longer you've worked on a story and the bigger the gap since you last looked at it;

- The more objective and self critical you've tried to be about it yourself;

- The more you're able to accept that you still have things to learn and that all books, no matter how good, can be improved;

- The more you've accepted that it's an integral and necessary part of the process of writing a good book;

- The more you read others' works and review them, and the more you learn about the craft of writing;

- The more objectively you can look at your own work and any criticism you may receive. More objective means with less emotional involvement;

- The more positive your attitude is towards criticism.

Think: Criticism is to help me make my work better. The more of it I get, the better I can make my writing. Don't think: If I get negative feedback, I'm a terrible writer.

The less hope or expectation that you have that the criticism is good, the less fearful and disappointed you'll be if it's not. Be realistic; there's going to be something they can pick you up on. Is there such a thing as a perfect book?

When you receive the feedback, look at it objectively, and if it's a valid point, act on it. The worst criticism, once acted on and fixed, might make the novel into something truly great. That's the exciting part. Fresh eyes see things clearly that are fuzzy to the authors because they're just too close. The potential is there for break-throughs.

With this attitude, you might even be disappointed if your beta readers have nothing bad to say.

Appendices

Keep in Touch

If you found any of this helpful, I'd be delighted if you could leave a review at your point of purchase. I really appreciate your time.

If you'd like to keep up with what I'm doing, sign up for my email list on the home page of my website, and I'll send you a free novel.

Visit my website and blog at http://tahlianewland.com

Follow '@Tahlia Newland' on Twitter.

Like 'TahliaNewland.artist.author.editor' on Facebook.

Be my fan on Goodreads.

My Fiction

You can see all my books with links to various purchase points on my website on the Book Shop page. Though they span genres and ages, the stories are all heart-warming and inspiring. Take a look at my latest, a metaphysical thriller; it's a great read for authors:

Prunella Smith: Worlds Within Worlds

'The barrier between the worlds shatters like the window. The beast is loose. My nightmare has become real. The guy has totally lost it. If he finds us here, we could die. No, I don't doubt it; we will die.'

Author and editor Prunella Smith inhabits a multilayered reality. Physically, she lives in the Australian bush with her crazy cat Merlin. In her work world, she edits the love story of Kelee, a Magan Lord's daughter, and in the cyber-world of social media, she's subjected to slanderous attacks by a disgruntled author. To complicate matters further, she sees things through the eyes of a Tibetan Yogi, has strange dreams and relives old memories.

Separate worlds, interconnected and complementary, but can they help when Prunella becomes victim to a real-life stalker and her sanity is threatened?

Worlds Within Worlds has a unique perspective on the nature of creativity. Its touch is light, its humour distinctive, but it reaches deep into the nature of human experience.

What readers are saying:

'This is riveting stuff, part magical realism dreamscape, part taut psychological thriller, and I was literally on the edge of my seat when the final twist—and what a twist it is—came around. Phew, what a ride! I can honestly say this is the best book I have read this year.' Frank Kusy, author of *Rupee Millionaire*.

'One of the most innovative and original works I have read in a long time. The book is compulsive enough to collapse time.' Richard Bunning Reviews.

'A contemplative story about the creative process that's also, amazingly, a page-turner. I put everything else aside and read it in a single afternoon.' Amazon Vine reviewer Dream Beast.

Buy it now. I'll be delighted if you do!

Other Books

The award-winning *Diamond Peak series*—young adult/new adult contemporary fantasy/magical realism. This visionary tale is an analogy for the journey to enlightenment.

A Matter of Perception—a collection of magical realism and urban fantasy short stories on the topic of perception.

A Hole in the Pavement—heart-warming ebook-only magical realism short story from the above collection.

You Can't Shatter Me—an inspiring and empowering young adult magical realism novel on the topic of how to handle a bully. Like *Lethal Inheritance*, the first book in the *Diamond Peak* series, this book has also won two awards, a BRAG Medallion for Outstanding Fiction and the AIA Seal of Excellence in Fiction.

You'll also find a range of quality books in a variety of genres on the Awesome Indies website: http://awesomeindies.net

About the Author

Tahlia Newland, author of the multi-award-winning Diamond Peak series, writes heart-warming magical realism. She has published six novels, one book of short stories and over 450 book reviews.

In 2012, she set up Awesome Indies Books, a review and accreditation service for independently published books, and is now merely part of a team that keeps it running. Tahlia has a Certificate in Editing and Proofreading and is a full time freelance editor specialising in structural editing and line editing. She also runs AIA Publishing, a selective author-funded publishing company.

Before turning to full time writing and editing, she had over twenty years' experience in scripting and performing in Visual Theatre and Theatre in Education. She is also a trained teacher with five years' experience in teaching high school creative and performing arts.

Tahlia is also a mask-maker and has had extensive training in meditation and Buddhist philosophy. She lives in Australia with a husband and a cheeky Burmese cat called George. Her adult daughter is a talented cover designer and film maker.

What the Awesome Indies Offers Authors

Awesome Indies Books (#AIbk) is an indie accreditation, review and book listing site. The books listed on the website have passed a stringent review process and have been Awesome Indies approved (AIA) by highly qualified reviewers as being the same, or of a higher, standard of craftsmanship as a mainstream published book. Only around 40% of books submitted to the Awesome Indies for accreditation meet the criteria. Another 10% meet it after revising their books to some degree; usually this involves another proof-read and sometimes a line edit.

Even books where their authors say they have been professionally edited do not always meet the criteria because the assessors look at all levels of editing. It's isn't a matter of having no typos; AI approval requires a high level of editing at all levels—developmental/structural editing, line editing, copyediting and proof-reading. Although the reviewers try to review submissions as objectively as possible—like a tutor marking an assignment or a publisher looking for their next book—where it isn't clear which side of the accreditation line a certain book lies, subjectivity does, of course, enter in to some degree. At this point you could say that the Awesome Indies has a 'house style', one that favours books that hold attention and have a strong voice and good

181

craftsmanship—you could call it accessible literary fiction, or genre fiction with literary sensibilities.

What does the Awesome Indies offer authors? Those whose books pass the scrutiny of our reviewers gain the confidence of knowing that their book is top quality—it's the same kind of validation that you get from a publishing deal. Those whose books just miss out, get advice for what they need to do to bring their work up to the required standard and, where desired, assistance in doing so. Authors who are prepared to look at their work again in light of the feedback get the most out of the submission process. If your book doesn't make the grade and the issues are too many for a quick fix, the aim is to give you enough feedback to help you to avoid the same problems in future books. Once authors have a book approved, it is listed on the Awesome Indies website, and the authors can join other Awesome Indies authors for marketing and general support.

Probably the best service is the One Stop Submission, where authors get the opinions of two highly qualified assessors for a minimal fee. The reviews are not published unless the author requests it, and the service can be used on unpublished books so long as the publication date is set. Many authors make a One Stop Submission part of their publication process. Whether used before or just after publication, you can tweak the book before it goes out to large numbers of people.

The Awesome Indies is always looking for qualified reviewers to join their team, so if you have qualifications in Creative Writing, English Literature, Journalism or editing and are interested in becoming an assessor for Awesome Indies approval, follow the relevant link on the front page of the website.

Lightning Source UK Ltd.
Milton Keynes UK
UKOW01f1832260516

275066UK00001B/16/P